Editorial

The Queen among Poets

In 1987 a group of Commonwealth writers met the Queen at the Commonwealth Institute in London to present her with an anthology. Carcanet had published *Under Another Sky: The Commonwealth Poetry Prize Anthology* which Alastair Niven edited. The prize had reached its fifteenth year, an occasion for celebration.

Niven took his title from Rajagopal Parthasarathy's poem 'Exile 2', commended in 1977:

> He had spent his youth whoring
> after English gods.
> There is something to be said for exile:
> you learn roots are deep.
> That language is a tree, loses colour
> under another sky

The prize, established in 1972, by 1987 was patronised by British Airways. They came on board, as it were, in 1985 when the rules were made more inclusive. Before, only poets writing in English from countries other than Great Britain could submit work. In 1985 poets from the British Isles, a growing number of them with roots in the Commonwealth and some of them not writing in English, were permitted to send in work. Niven's anthology includes winning and commended poems from each year of the Prize.

The first winner was Chinua Achebe, who attended the event at the Institute. Because the judges were in disagreement, that first award was shared with the Canadian George McWhirter. On only one other occasion did disagreement yield a split prize. Subsequent winners were Wayne Brown from Trinidad, Dennis Scott from Jamaica, and a distinguished list of men (David Dabydeen, Vikram Seth twice, Michael Longley, Niyi Osundare and Iain Crichton Smith among them). In 1980 Shirley Lim, the first woman and the first Malaysian, was chosen, and soon the glass ceiling was further breached by Grace Nichols, Lauris Edmond, Vicki Raymond and Lorna Goodison. Grace Nichols contributed an 'Epilogue' to our book:

> I have crossed an ocean
> I have lost my tongue
> from the root of the old one
> a new one has sprung

The Queen moved among a great press of poets drawn from all over the world, exchanging words and smiles. She had a proper conversation with Chinua Achebe who stood to my right. As publisher, it fell to me to present her with a copy of the book. I told her that I might be the only Mexican publisher in her dominions. 'Mexican?' she smiled, 'you don't *look* Mexican.'

I write this as we await news from Balmoral. I was remembering another occasion to which I cannot put a date. Carol Ann Duffy as poet laureate had prevailed upon her Majesty to invite a gaggle, ascension, ambush, aurora, assembly – what is the collective noun, or is this a gap in our language? – of poets to Buckingham Palace for drinks and canapes. The palace had put on display a number of the poetic treasures from the royal archive. The one I best remember is the copy of George Herbert's *The Temple* which Charles I was reading the night before his execution. Again her Majesty, now a good deal older, moved among the poets. A few of us hoary male writers were gathered to hold a conversation with her, which we did. Then, as I walked around enjoying the opulence, a voice hissed, 'Schmidt!' It was Geoffrey Hill, sitting apart. He had had enough. 'Get me out of here,' he said, and that's what I did. I took his elbow and led him down to the street. And afterwards, I couldn't get back in.

Kenward Elmslie (1929–2022) • *Miles Champion writes:* The poetry community has lost one of its most loadbearing yet unobtrusive pillars: the librettist, poet, publisher and songwriter Kenward Elmslie died peacefully of natural causes at his home in Manhattan's West Village on 29 June; he was ninety-three. Elmslie's publications span forty-plus years, from *Pavilions* (Tibor de Nagy, 1961) to *Agenda Melt* (Adventures in Poetry, 2004). From the get-go, his poetry manifests a gloriously sui generis quality; skittish and vehement by turns, and as ordered as it is deranged, it gives the lie to the notion that abstract poetry doesn't actually *say* anything. His play, *City Junket*, based on Henri Rousseau's *Une visite à l'exposition de 1899*, was the first to be staged by the Eye and Ear Theater Company, in 1979, with sets by Red Grooms; his novel, *The Orchid Stories*, is one of the indelible prose works of the last fifty years.

A lifelong devotee of musicals and opera, Elmslie wrote the lyrics for Claibe Richardson's cult classic *The Grass Harp* (based on Truman Capote's novel) and the librettos for, among others, Ned Rorem's *Miss Julie* and Jack Beeson's *The Sweet Bye and Bye* and *Lizzie Borden*. His early song 'Love-Wise' was recorded by Nat King Cole in 1959. *Lingoland*, the revue he assembled in 2005 featuring his songs, poems and dialogues, was a life-affirming joy that offered far more than could reasonably be asked of an off-Broadway night out (look for it on CD, CDJAY2 1395).

For decades Elmslie divided his time between New York City and Calais (pronounced 'callous'), Vermont. Elmslie's partner and collaborator of thirty years, Joe Brainard, wrote *I Remember* in Elmslie's Calais farmhouse, and Elmslie founded Z Press there, publishing books by John Ashbery, Edwin Denby, Barbara Guest and Harry Mathews, among others, as well as six issues of an annual magazine (*Z* through *ZZZZZZ*, 1973–78). An affable and entertaining – if eccentric – resident of the town, the dirt road he lived on was named Elmslie Road in the 1970s.

A Pulitzer heir – his grandfather was Joseph Pulitzer – Elmslie's numerous charitable gifts to artists, writers, civil rights groups and community organisations were as generous as they were anonymous. He was larger than life, with a fine baritone singing voice. The mould for his like no longer exists, alas; he cannot and will not be replaced.

SONG

carnations
tangerines
let's walk a little ways

and when the fruits are mushy
a hoverer
will give us a haven

pop art rose
impressionist potato flower
let's walk a little ways

and when the plastic browns
a machinist
will coat us all with greensward

Portugal's beloved radical daughter Ana Luísa Amaral, poet and translator of Dickinson and Shakespeare (1956–2022) • She was a poet of specifics, of motherhood, of 'all the worlds that are in this world' and, as a Portuguese obituarist wrote, of the diminutive that contains the universal. She also helped introduce gender studies in Portuguese universities. She died – untimely – of cancer and is survived by her daughter and her mother. Her poetry has been widely published in English, a third collection, *World*, due out next year. She was a wonderful performer, by heart, of her own and others' poems, and her voice is preserved alongside her texts. Her translation of 300 of Emily Dickinson's poems are said to be particularly accomplished. Her first collection was a substantial success and she was soon among the best-loved poets of modern Portugal. She received the Reina Sofía Prize for her work. In her last book, published earlier this year in a bilingual Portuguese/Spanish edition (she has a substantial readership in Spain), 'her protagonists are a centipede which with difficulty scales the bathroom wall; the bee which "methodical and happy", tastes the nectar of the flowers; or that parti-coloured magpie'.

She built on and strengthened the long link between Portuguese and British culture, teaching British and American Literature at the University of Oporto and responding to the poets of the eighteenth as well as the later, more popular centuries. The obituarist in *El País* speaks of how her sense of solidarity marked her life as it does her work – a solidarity which is not hectoring but particular. No wonder her work exists in fifteen languages beyond her own. Whether swatting a mosquito or braving the waves with Odysseus, writing about the experience of migrants or a recipe or a priest's pain at some of the Bible scenes, her world is particularly alive.

A 'Native Alien' Poet, cricketer & novelist (1935–2022) • Zulfikar Ghose died in July at the age of eighty-seven. Born in India, he arrived in Britain in 1952, settling in London. The poet-to-be attended Keele University, reading English and Philosophy. He became a reckonable figure on the London poetry and critical scene, forming with experimental novelist B.S. Johnson and poet Anthony Smith a sub-set of 'the Group', metropolitan successors to 'the Movement'. He received a Gregory Award for his poetry in 1963 and existed as a schoolmaster and freelance writer. Not least among his enthusiasms was cricket, about which he wrote for the *Observer*. He also reviewed books. His first book of poems came in 1964 (*The Loss of India*) and his autobiographical *Confessions of a Native Alien* the year after. He also wrote a dozen novels, several non-fiction books and six further collections of poetry. He abandoned the British in 1969 and thereafter taught creative writing in the United States. An initial one-year contract grew into a thirty-eight-year commitment.

Cuba's long-heard voice, another radical (1923–2022) • Fina García Marruz was ninety-nine years old when she died in Havana at the end of June, one of the long-serving poets of Latin America and specifically of Cuba, of several Cubas. She was not only a poet: she was an essayist and a critic of moment. She received the major literary awards of her own country, but also in 2011 the Lorca Prize of the City of Granada. In the same year she was awarded the Reina Sofía Prize, the supreme accolade.

The Casa de las Américas regretted the loss of 'one of the most extraordinary poetic voices of Latin America'. It reminded readers that she was a founding member of the *Orígenes* group that centred around the eponymous magazine (1944–56) and included Wilfredo Lam, José Lezama Lima and foreign contributors – Juan Ramón Jiménez, Aimé Césaire, Paul Valéry, Vicente Aleixandre, Albert Camus, Luis Cernuda, Paul Claudel, Paul Éluard, Gabriela Mistral, Octavio Paz, Alfonso Reyes and Theodore Spencer among them. She taught at the University of Havana where she received awards for her essays and critical writing. She was a leading expert on the work of Cuba's national poet José Martí and was part of the editorial team that produced his *Obras Completas*. Prensa Latina called her 'one of the greatest voices not only of Cuban but of world poetry', who had survived attempts from various quarters to silence and marginalise her voice. The president of Cuba added his voice to the chorus of praise and reminded the world that the North American blockade of Cuba was in its seventh decade, but the country continues and, in its unique way, thrives.

Joie de vivre and fantasy • *Geoffrey Pawling writes*: Tony Mitton, one of Britain's most popular and versatile children's poets, died in June this year aged 71. As a Cambridge undergraduate he studied under J.H. Prynne, but

ballad and song were so central to Mitton's love of poetry that the work of more traditional contemporary poets, most of all Charles Causley, provided the bearings he needed.

Over the last thirty years Mitton's poetry, published in colourful books of all shapes and sizes, has delighted very young listeners and readers with its fizzing wit and playfulness, while at least two collections of his poems for older children sit well with the classics of that genre. In *Plum* (1998) and *Come into This Poem (2011)* the traditional resources of poetry are deployed in a variety of forms – there is even a memorable villanelle – but also consort with the most contemporary idiom, as in 'Txt PoM'. Then there is the range of subjects, as a run of just three poems from *Plum* suggest: 'Nits', 'The Hag of Beara', 'Awakening' (the Buddha's meditation under the Bhodi tree). But above all Mitton's poetry celebrates domestic life and the natural world. He could make even a garden snail glamorous, giving it the full Keatsian treatment ("Nightwriter").

Among Mitton's other notable works are his prize-winning *Wayland*, retelling the Norse legend in ballad form, and his novel *Potter's Boy*. A number of his poems for young children have inspired musical accompaniment for performances by the City of Birmingham Symphony and the Hallé Orchestras, the latest of these collaborations being performed by the Hallé to altogether more than 2200 children at two concerts held only days after Mitton died. For the Hallé too he wrote the words for *Goddess Gaia*, Steve Pickett's cantata for flute, harp, cello and narrator. Words and music, the music of words, that kinship was very dear to Tony Mitton.

Lonesome Cowboy (1945–2022) • Baxter Black, the cowboy poet, a recognised voice on National Public Radio and a celebrated performer, has departed his home on the range. He reached the pinnacle of cowboy Parnassus, as grand marshal of the National Western Stock Show parade in Denver in 2009. He was commentator on the event for more than ten years. His *New York Times* obituarist Clay Risen described him as a writer and speaker 'whose witty, big-hearted verse about cowpokes, feed lots and wide-open vistas elevated the tradition of Western doggerel to something of a folk art'. His widow Cindy Lou Black said he died of leukaemia. His death outed the fact that poetry is rife among cowboys: 'more than 100 cowboy poetry festivals are held each year, and the peripatetic Mr. Black was often featured as the main event'. Clay Risen continues: 'And, he said, cowboy poetry is fun. Forget intimations of immortality; Mr. Black's poetry cracked wise about things like horse manure, the evils of vegetarianism and the advantages of artificial preservatives...' Well-known, well-loved, he was also widely published, with over sixty books to his name. 'I count myself very lucky that I get to be a part of the wonderful world of horse sweat, soft noses, close calls and twilight on the trail,' he wrote. 'I like living a life where a horse matters.'

Poetry as Panacea • When poets are elevated to prominent civic positions, they are invited to talk in sweeping generalities and platitudes. The new American Poet Laureate Ada Limón, the twenty-fourth writer to occupy that post, is a reckonable poet. From her new eyrie, she proposes poetry as panacea for all our problems. In July, asked, 'what can poetry offer a divided country?' she replied: 'Yeah. I think that it's really important to remember that even in this particularly hard moment, divided moment, poetry can really help us reclaim our humanity. And I think it's important right now at a time when so many of us have been numbed to trauma, to grief, to chaos. And so many of us have had to compartmentalize in order to live our lives. And we've had to kind of forget, conveniently, that we are thinking, feeling, grieving, emotional beings. And I think through poetry, I think we can actually remember that on the other side of that is also contentment, joy, a little peace now and again, and that those are all part of the same spectrum. And without one, we don't have the other. And I think poetry is the place where we can go to break open. But to have that experience, I really, truly believe helps us remember that we're human. And reclaiming our humanity seems like it's really essential right now.'

Addition and Subtraction • In June, the GCSE syllabus was redrawn to include poetry by Ilya Kaminsky, Louise Bennet-Coverley, Caleb Femi, Raymond Antrobus, Warsan Shire and Theresa Lola. This enhances the variety of poets on offer to GCSE candidates. They will no longer be required to grapple with Keats, Hardy, Owen, Larkin, Heaney or Sassoon. In the circumstances, quoting 'Dockery and Son' out of context (in the poet's centenary year) seems apposite:

> Why did he think adding meant increase?
> To me it was dilution. Where do these
> Innate assumptions come from? Not from what
> We think truest, or most want to do:
> Those warp tight-shut, like doors.

Nadhim Zahawi, the then Education Secretary, called the decision 'cultural vandalism'. 'I will be speaking to the exam board to make this clear,' he said. His time is over. Surely he might have acknowledged that greater diversity in the poetry offered to students should be welcomed. It is only sad that the OCR Exam Board did not opt for 'dilution', adding without subtraction; and that the talk was more about poems than poets. It is probably outrageous that 'An Arundel Tomb' and 'Anthem for Doomed Youth' have been binned: but what has been put in their place? The Board explained that it wanted to 'replace some Victorian and 20th-century poems which have either become overfamiliar through the assessment process, or which have proved to have unexpected difficulties or seemed less accessible for students'. The GCSE anthology contains forty-five poems. fifteen were culled, fifteen were added. 'Of the 15 poets whose work has been added to GCSE English literature, 14 are poets of colour. Six are Black women, one is of south Asian heritage. Our new poets also include disabled and LGBTQ+ voices.'

Rupi Kaur on Education • Rupi Kaur has not yet made it on to the GCSE or A-level syllabus (though her books have been banned from schools in Texas), but she has told her 4.5 million Instagram followers that the widely-reported plans to remove or reduce the English Literature and Creative Writing element in some universities is 'horrible' and made her feel 'sad'. Her debut book sold eight million copies. She declared that studying English literature shaped what she did as a writer and she was unhappy that others might not be able to have the same experience at undergraduate level. The universities currently planning cuts and changes include Sheffield Hallam University, Roehampton and Wolverhampton. Kaur is currently on a world tour that takes in the United Kingdom. Speaking to Sky News, she said she finds readings energising: 'I'm totally engaged and having conversations throughout the whole show, and that's what makes performing so magical. It kind of just feels like a giant sleepover with all of your besties!'

Prizes Wane • In its 21 July editorial, the *Bookseller* spoke of the book trade's anxiety as some of the major prizes are postponed or closed down. 'Prize organisers are increasingly concerned by the difficulty of attracting sponsors in economically straitened times, with others worried books are not valued by wider society, influencing the decisions of potential corporate backers. This summer, the UK has seen a spate of worrying announcements from established prizes. In June, the Costa Book Awards were cancelled with no warning and no explanation. Within weeks, the Blue Peter Award was also scrapped. [...] This was followed by warnings that the *Sunday Times* Short Story Award could be discontinued following the loss of Audible as a sponsor, and the announcement that the Desmond Elliott Prize will not run in 2023...'

Prizes won: Feltrinelli Poetry Prize 2022: €250,000 • Michael Longley received one of the major European poetry prizes, the 2022 Feltrinelli International Prize for Poetry. Every five years the Accademia dei Lincei in Rome makes the award. Previous winners include W.H. Auden, Eugenio Montale and John Ashbery.

The Accademia dei Lincei accolade declares: 'Longley is an extraordinary poet of landscape, particularly of the Irish West, which he observes with the delicate and passionate attention of an ecologist, and a tragic singer of Ireland and its dramatic history. But with his poetry he has also addressed the seduction, conquest, and fascination of love, as well as the shock of war in all ages, the tragedy of the Holocaust and of the gulags, and the themes of loss, grief and pity. For the extraordinary relevance of his themes and their cultural implications, as well as the very high stylistic quality of his oeuvre, the 2022 Antonio Feltrinelli International Prize for Poetry is awarded to Michael Longley.'

Longley will accept the prize at a ceremony at the Accademia in Rome in November. He has previously received the T.S. Eliot Prize, the Hawthornden Prize, the *Irish Times* Poetry Now Award, the American Ireland Fund Literary Award and the Griffin International Prize.

Reports

Touch and Mourning

Part 1: See You at the Funeral

ANTHONY VAHNI CAPILDEO

This essay was written in an unhugged state, indoors, in the tropical dry season. Revisiting it under trees, in Greyfriars kirkyard, in the Scottish summer, I am more hugged, but in a selective way. This is a summer of dodging and flinching. Pat, pat, pat. Variant clinches. Yet here is a coronavirus pandemic paradox. The closest I have been to any body, any bodies, was the proximity shimmering off the screen like a heatwave, during the Zoom funeral for Miss Rosalind Wilson, my former English teacher at St Joseph's Convent, Port of Spain. Trinidad and Tobago's government had made a serious attempt to contain the mutation of the virus and injury to the population. There were no more than six masked, distanced mourners physically present at the funeral. Those of us wanting to be present online were confronted with the swept, near-empty church – not the rainbow-glass school chapel – through a fixed camera, which showed the side of the coffin, and an angled view of the altar. However, there was an unexpected kind of presence.

In the Zoom squares, we saw a tessellation of each other's faces: 'Convent girls' from across eight decades. Was this intimacy, or violation? At a funeral, especially a Trinidad funeral, I expect to be hyper-aware of living bodies. There would be scents of cocoa butter, coconut oil, talcum powder, French and American perfumes, ironed cotton, overly sunned nylon, lilies, chrysanthemums. We would hug and cry uncomfortably, consolingly; nobody a stranger. Jaws would press into shoulders; handbags would wallop hips. We would feel a trembling throughout the congregation; glimpse handkerchiefs in our peripheral vision; see the altar vessels shine through our tears. In the Roman Catholic Mass, we would be creaking and kneeling, getting up and sitting down, out of time with each other, and in synch. Above all, we would not be seeing each other's faces; not with the fixity of Zoom. We would not have to contemplate the older Convent girls' frozen, furrowed dignity, used to downfacing colonial examinations and transgenerational trauma. We would not have to see the squashy-faced tears of today's school gate mothers.

What to do with this presence? In the altering conditions of lockdown, or since; wherever you happen to be, have you attended Zoom funerals? Have you, too, turned to the chat box as a kind of telepathic community of mourning? Instead of nudging up for space in the pews or helping someone less able to walk, we exchanged tips on solving technical problems; we typed out the prayer responses we might say; we shared the reflections that,

at an in-person funeral, would have passed, with the silence of fish, in our dark minds, unuttered. The mourners filed out of the church. The camera was left running. The senior priest, with no help – no concelebrants, no altar servers, no formidable church ladies – like an aged bear, slowly, simply, cleared up after the sacrifice. This gentle housework was his job.

Zoom funerals: another of those pandemic liberations. What liberation? If the wider 'normality' is the world consciousness of memes and strategic planning, the liberation is into the time-worn, honourable normality of the diasporic, the disabled, the incarcerated, and the enclosed. Singing and weeping were paired by Boccaccio. Poetic heritage, embodiment and incarceration are a triple-threaded theme, in Terrance Hayes's *American Sonnets for My Past and Future Assassin* (Penguin, 2018).

> I lock you in an American sonnet that is part prison,
> Part panic closet, a little room in a house set aflame.
> I lock you in a form that is part music box, part meat
> Grinder to separate the song of the bird from the bone.

Can we be liberated into sharing the normality where the most loved may be the furthest? Liberated into the intensification of yearning, embracing through eyes, voice, and technology (if you are so lucky)?

The distant-often-not-by-choice are ever with us. To love is to love *towards*. Zohar Atkins, a great poet of yearning and wisdom (with flashes of mortal irreverence), begins his 'Without Without Title' (*Nineveh*, Carcanet, 2019):

> A poem that admits there is no meaning
> besides the gathering of syllables
> into little bouquets of desire,
> placed, somewhere, between light and dust,
> is said to need, as water needs,
> the beauty of visible breath. If
> wisdom is not to be had, it is to be sung.

I was hopeful that the pandemic would bring about such an uncommon liberation into a more common humanity. At last, 'we' would become 'them', at least for a time. This, perhaps, is why the dance of virus denial proceeds with such fury. A fury of disidentification with otherness; a repudiation of that season of resembling (if not remembering) the forgotten. Ever with us.

Now there is the fury of the identification vs. otherness

in the wake of the passing of the extraordinary Queen Elizabeth II. Some mourners focus on Her Majesty the suffering individual, bravely performing the length of a dutiful life. These mourners can find themselves released into grieving, remembering their own lost elders in a way they might not have permitted themselves at the time. Death can have a face, familiar and beloved. Some mourners remember their own lost elders, lost because of the horrors of Empire. These mourners of the unnumbered are familiar with the face of the Crown as part of a dynasty of portraits and statues, and stamped upon money, divinizing, or raising up, certain humans at the expense of others. Thus, any royal passing inevitably brings up centuries of deaths. My friar friends, in an appreciative

homily, prayed humbly for God's help with 'whatever work still has to be done in her soul' for her to see Him fully – a reminder that the kingdom of heaven is our attempt to make heaven on earth in how we lovingly behold, accompany, sometimes hold each other – a true attempt, and also impossible in this life.

I stay hopeful, post-pandemic, that so many people having met friends online as if they would not meet again, will understand how 'not meeting again' becomes a background colour to 'other' lives: a forever tone, though not a saturating glare or darkness. How fondness is a work of perseverance, not reactivity or liking: a dear stone warming in the pocket above your heart, not the gleaming prick of a pin badge.

On Sappho: Reading Lyric Fragments

KYOKA HADANO

This piece was first published in *The Isis,* a publication at the University of Oxford.

We are strangely drawn to bits and pieces. The blunted shimmer of sea-glass, newspaper clippings, crumbling broken hazelnuts atop a cake. But what if we were thinking about fragmentary language? Words ending mid-sentence

>] random indentation
> grammar eluded

dissolve our expectations of lexical coherence. Teased out of the cohesion of sense and sentence, we find ourselves riddled with interruptions, lacunae, punctured openings, and unhemmed endings.

Sappho's poetry is one of fragmentation. Intentional or not, her writings have remained with us in bits and pieces, preserved as citations in the works of other ancient authors or inscribed on strips of frayed papyri. Of the nine books of lyric poetry she is said to have composed, only one poem has reached us in its complete state. In the rare case that papyri *do* survive without significant damage, they still make for problematic reading: text is written upon them in columns, without word division, punctuation, or lineation. The very act of reading – even in this primary editorial phase – is one of piecing together the gaps.

This broken form chimes well with Sappho's prevailing poetic theme of unrequited desire. The lover always yearns for what they do not have, and Sappho's lyrical 'I' is no exception, for whom love unreciprocated is a condition predicated on absence. Having recently thumbed through the pages of the writer and classicist Anne Carson's essay collection *Eros the Bittersweet*, I recall her observation that '[t]he Greek word 'eros' denotes 'want,'

'lack,' 'desire for that which is missing''. Such is the condition of Sappho's lyrics, which evoke love as a yearning for what is not there, absences brought into relief by scenic displacements. Carson's interpretation of Sappho's Greek is also an imagining of this distant realm:

I long and seek after (fr. 36)

Moon has set
And Pleiades huddle
Night, the hour goes by,
Alone I lie. (fr. 168B)

Reading her fragments this way is a process of re-composition – the absences of the text coax forward the presence of the reader. Punning on the gaps in the text of Sappho's corpus, the scholar Yopie Prins proposes that '[r]eading Sappho is a form of riddling'. She suggests that '[w]hen we read the fragments, we ask a question about voice that we answer by projecting voice into the[m].' This question-and-answer movement of 'projecting voice' suggests that reading is a sort of interiorised dialogue: a conversation with, and through, the text before us. The act of deciphering 'Sappho' from the crumbled array of words before us is a demand to make sense of characters on the page, to pay careful attention to calibrations of context and ornament. The intimacy of this process – of reading, of translating, of (re)composition – aligns the reader to the figure of the lover, as Carson writes:

Eros is always a story in which lover, beloved and the difference between them interact. The interaction is a fiction arranged by the mind of the lover. It carries an emotional charge both hateful and delicious, and emits a light like knowledge.[1]

This account could just as well be ascribed to the reader and editor of Sappho's poetry, invited as we are to tease meaning out of these silences in her oeuvre. It is through the act of readerly interpretation – of resting our fingertips along a poem's ragged edges and contemplating that which may have been lost – that unlocks what Plato's Socrates describes as the process of 'heal[ing] the wound of human nature'.[2] Through literary love, lyric can be completed, an undeniable link between Sappho's writing of desire and the readerly desire for 'Sappho' as poet.

In this way, she is the lyric poet of 'eros' par excellence, inviting, through a history of material loss, her readers into piecing back together the trailing lines. Consider fragment 21 (à la Carson):

]
]
]pity
]trembling
]
]flesh by now old age
]covers
]flies in pursuit
]
]noble
]taking
]sing to us
The one with violets in her lap
]mostly
]goes astray

Carson's typographical choice of using squared brackets in translation indicates destroyed sections of the manuscripts, or unclear characters, 'an aesthetic gesture towards the papyrological event', in her own words. She thus encodes and accentuates the silences whorled in the fabric of the poems by weaving together a filigree of lovelorn asymmetries. The seventeenth-century writer George Puttenham described these purposeful gaps in rhetorical terms as 'the figure of silence' or 'aposiopesis', the term for an abrupt breaking off in speech.[3] The gaps' texture is akin to that of rest-signs in sheet music, or the pauses for effect given in an oratory speech.

But instead of visual prompts, we are looking at words, shimmering and inchoate, mediated by lexical deciphering and scholarly remediation. Amidst a poem peppered with these ambiguities, the only line in fragment 21 which survives in its entirety is an enigmatic reference to 'the one with violets in her lap'. In the endnotes to the volume, Carson admits with readerly deference that 'I do not know what this adjective means exactly'. The adjective ('ἰόκολπον' in Greek) is a compound word, from 'ion', meaning 'violet' ('purple' or 'dark' or 'like violets' are other options) and the word 'kolpos', for which Carson gives many possible meanings: 'bosom, lap, womb, fold formed by a loose garment; any hollow.' Carson also notes that, in Sappho, the dusky purples of violets are 'an epithet of brides and of a goddess' and this fact conjures in my mind other similar referents across her oeuvre. Is this reference to 'violets' in fragment 21 the same as that of fragment 30: 'girls [...] might sing of the love between you and the bride / with violets in her lap' or of fragment 103: ']child of Kronos with violets in her lap'? Interweaving the images of 'a child of Kronos', jealous 'anger' and 'the bride', I wonder whether Sappho is hinting Hera to us, wife of Zeus and the goddess of marriage. This could imply – I twirl my pen at my desk as I write this, quietly proud of my literary sleuth work – that some of these songs were 'epithalamiums', wedding poems.

There seems to be a sad irony in the idea of lovers twinned à deux, who are however – over the contingencies of time and history – torn away from one another, only to be pieced back together in the realms of ambiguous obscurity. For, after all, fragments are also ruins. They imply something left behind from what had once been a whole.

Yet such an interpretation – of course – is only in the realms of readerly conjecture. The nature of fragments, from an author no longer breathing and before us, diffracts and unlocks a plethora of potential meanings from a text. Where anyone can have their own unique reading of a text, sometimes necessarily mediated in translation, fragments create a conversation between ourselves and the forms the words cast before us. Through these intertwined threads of interpretation, reader and the lover together become 'mythoplokon' ('weavers of fictions' (fragment 188)).

These fragmented translations of Sappho encode an admission of frailty – their very form is suggestive of the compositional process, the fraying away of words by time and memory, the incoherent passion of a lover's confession, its flickering impressions. And yet, there is something in tears and aches that invites sympathy. The critic Virginia Jackson writes about how we define lyric poetry not in terms of fixed taxonomies, but as a way of reading or 'lyricisation'.[4] Through the process of lyric reading, of pausing our fingertips upon a poetic fragment and slipping closed the knots of imperfection, we can tend to these poetic wounds and re-calibrate our understanding of the broken condition as something in fact complete.

NOTES

[1] Carson, *Eros the Bittersweet*, p. 169.

[2] Plato, 'Symposium', in *Lysis. Symposium. Gorgias*, trans. by W.R.M. Lamb (Cambridge: MA: Harvard University Press, 1925),192e (pp. 144–5).

[3] George Puttenham, *The Arte of English Poesie* (London: Triphook, 1811), p. 139.

[4] Virginia Jackson, *Dickinson's Misery* (Princeton, NJ: Princeton University Press, 2005), p. 6

Something there Is

J. KATES

I live in rural, southwestern New Hampshire, and sometimes I write poems. This inevitably leads to comparisons, and a constant fear that my own writing will be taken, the way a dean at my university once characterized another poet, as 'when the Frost is on the bumpkin'. Indeed, Robert Frost's work was one welcoming gateway for me into modern poetry, and I have always appreciated the multiplicity within his work, reading him not as the 'Saturday Evening Post philosopher' Gregory Corso once took him for, 'but such as plagiarizes God'. And it was Richard Wilbur who first introduced me – with a brilliant essay in which he read 'Birches' 'as a rejection of the sort of soaring idealism we find in Shelley' – to how much of Frost's poetry is underpinned by a conscious conversation with other writers. If you don't believe Wilbur or me, look at 'The Most of It' side by side with Wordsworth's 'There was a Boy...' Or, from the other side, read Wendell Berry's 'Stay Home' after Frost's 'The Pasture'.

This spring, I have been clearing and rebuilding a stone wall around my house. It marks no boundary, simply the abandoned ruin of some early breeder of Merino sheep. (These walls were constructed for the most part during the early nineteenth century, and they thread now along roads and through abandoned fields into fully grown woodlands. Some of them marked boundaries, as Frost contemplated.) Mine surrounds a couple of acres within the property, and, every fall, the leaves drift up against its eastern side, composting into soil, rooting blueberries, turning parts of the wall into drifting ramps. I don't mind the blueberries, but I'm not sentimental about those – I have plenty more. Something in me needs the wall to be a wall, its own artefact.

So.

I have been raking out dead leaves, uprooting shrubbery, digging out stones that have been long obscured, even conducting a little involuntary archaeology: Who left that brown glass bottle buried now so far underground? The original wall had to be at least four feet high to contain the sheep. In places now it rises barely a foot or two above the ground. The foundations are deep. Rocks that have fallen off, or those that were never on but are still close enough, I pry out with a rusted shovel and heave on top of the lower courses. They will stand out for the next couple of years by the difference in colour, khaki tan or deep brown against the weathered gray of the wall itself. But not for long.

This is an absolutely useless activity. Few people visit me, and those who do don't notice or care about the outskirts of my clearing. It's exercise, sure, and I can get far more and varied exercise by clearing trails in the woods, splitting wood, or simply walking to the lake. But day after day this April I have been out there, raking away dead leaves, hefting stones far larger than my head, grubbing soil.

The only aesthetic pleasure is my own, looking out of a window and seeing what I have done. That feels good, in passing.

If there is any immanent virtue, it is in communing with the past and the future. Somehow, I am continuing or reaffirming or at the very least acknowledging the work of that sheep farmer – like a member of the congregation adding my 'amen' to the preacher's homily – and stabilizing the wall for the appreciation (or not) of those who will come after me. It's nothing but a conversation in time.

It's what Frost taught me to do in his poetry, and in mine. Seamus Heaney felt this as a family activity, but for me there's no kinship in it, it's a more abstract communion.

By any measure, I'm a minor poet. My poems as far as I can tell make nothing happen. A few people read them and compliment me, as a neighbour might stop and admire my stone-wall industry; and I certainly feel good as I write. (I learned long ago that the elation on writing a bad poem is exactly the same as the elation on writing a good one. Only time will tell whether the rock will hold or tumble.) When I write, I am writing in correspondence with those who have come before me, and in a hopeful, hopefully uncontrollable correspondence with those who will come after.

Christopher Fiore taught me literature and writing in high school. Raised in working-class Homestead, Pennsylvania, and never a poet himself, he was among the first to encourage me, and one of the strongest critics of what I wrote. We became friends. I gave him a sapling cherry ('loveliest of trees...') on the birth of his daughter. In my early twenties when I despaired that I had earned only about one hundred dollars from my writing, he wrote back, 'How many people in the world can claim to have earned a hundred dollars from their own writing?' That my poems have always been grounded in the real world is partly due to his pedagogic influence, although my affinity for country life is rooted in a deeper stratum. A few years ago, I wrote an occasional poem for him in a cadence perhaps more borrowed than stolen. I was gratified he was able to hear his wife read it to him before he died.

A THANK-YOU NOTE: TAKEN DOUBLY
or, the Gratitude of Influence

The wall was there before I owned the land,
composed of stones as random as the glacier
had laid them down millennia before,
but placed as carefully balanced as a poet
might take the words found littering at hand
and build into a line he meant to last
if not all time, at least a life or two.

At times one vision gets into your head,
at other times another. I can't help looking
at waterlilies through a Frenchman's eyes

or sunsets through a bilious Englishman's.
It's hard to walk the acres deeded me
without conceding that they're you-know-whose
as much as they're the turkeys' and the bear's.

But if I give that older poet his due,
I have another debt to keep in mind,

and that's to you, my teacher and my friend,
as everything we own is filtered through
the words of those who taught us how to see
and spell the objectivity of rock
like Merlin moving mountains to make Stonehenge
or one poor farmer clearing what he can.

Letter from Wales

SAM ADAMS

The notion of a collection of essays exploring contemporary Welsh identities arose from discussions involving Darren Chetty, Elan Grug Muse, Hanan Issa and Iestyn Tyne at the Hay festival in 2019 about the need to pose again the questions Raymond Williams asked (in *Welsh Culture)* back in 1975, 'Where is the real identity, the real culture' of Wales? It is clear that, as editors, the four invited a personal response from contributors, and that is what we find in *Welsh [Plural] – Essays on the Future of Wales* (Repeater, 2022). But the title is misleading: nowhere among the contents is there a vision of the future. Almost all the writers have a present grievance, be it with the condition of Wales as a nation of the United Kingdom, or shockingly common manifestations of racism in Welsh daily life.

The collection showcases some familiar names, including the novelists Jo Dunthorne and Niall Griffiths, the former admitting to pronouncing 'tooth' like 'tuth', as any phonetically sensible person would, while Griffiths, an altogether thornier character, skewers 'the hollow men in London' and the Welsh Tory leader who said, 'Wales is sleepwalking towards independence' with vitriolic rejoinders. Historian Martin Johnes writes of the common perception of a subjugated Wales which, though not entirely lacking supporting evidence, is difficult to uphold when hundreds of thousands of our contemporaries have either recently arrived from England or have English ancestry. 'Dismissive and patronising' attitudes to our language and notions of nationhood may make the blood boil, he says, but what really matters is the marginalisation of the Welsh economy by successive Westminster governments. The evidence for this is plain to see when I return to roots in Gilfach Goch and witness how that community, vibrant in my youth, has been hollowed out. Elsewhere in the Valleys, public libraries and halls, and ranks of shops, stand closed and often ruinous. All this because much of industrial south Wales was shut down without thought, certainly without planning, for the consequences.

And now, in Dyffryn Nantlle, her north Wales home, Grug Muse observes changes at street level under the onslaught of the digital economy and on-line delivery services – 'the banks close. And the butcher's. And the

hardware store'. Much of rural Wales is in decline or already 'changed utterly' as EU farming subsidies have not been replaced since Brexit and the farms that remain face competition from cheaper imports. She sees about her in Gwynedd a battleground in which rural gentrification is winning the day – with unanticipated knock-on effects. The deracinated Welsh speakers, displaced from their heartlands, seek out employment and homes in rundown parts of Cardiff, setting in motion another gentrification process. Elsewhere, published statistics throw light on what may appear anomalous, that at a 2020 survey there were more Welsh speakers in Cardiff (89,700) than in Gwynedd (89,200). But those figures represent 11 percent of the population of the capital, of whom 12 percent claim to speak Welsh daily, while in Gwynedd 75 percent of the population are able to speak Welsh and 65 percent use the language daily.

Iestyn Tyne sees the livelihoods of hill farming families in catastrophic decline, arguing it is clear evidence that the devolution settlement has not gone far enough. He contends that to retain the strong backbone of vital familial and community structures and the Welsh language that belongs with them, Wales must look to independence. Dan Evans's scholarly critique of modern Wales, 'Reconstructing Welshness – Again', draws similar conclusions. It characterises current political narratives of Welshness as 'unionistic... imperialistic... white, macho and elite led', and not reflective of the views of the majority of the population. For him, the veneer of political autonomy afforded to the Welsh Assembly in Cardiff has not succeeded in countering economic dependency. Further, remarkable as they are, advances in Welsh-language education in more populous areas cannot make up for the reduction in numbers of Welsh speakers in the predominantly rural heartlands of the north and west. Communities where in their daily routines over 50 percent of the population speak Welsh, pumping Welshness through to the rest of us, have become, he says, mere 'husks' as their young people leave, often because property prices, driven by increasing second-home ownership, rise beyond the reach of locals. That was how things stood when Tyne was writing his essay. At the beginning of July 2022, however, three years on from its composition, the Welsh government announced imminent changes to regulations that will allow local planning authorities in Wales to control the number of second homes and holiday lets in their area and local councils to increase council tax premiums on second and empty homes 'to give everyone *yr hawl i fyw adra* – the right to live at home, that is, 'to live and work in the communities in which they grew up'.

Shaheen Sutton was born and brought up not far from where I write, in the Pillgwenlly area of Newport, which is 'ethnically, culturally and religiously diverse', as was reflected in her schooling alongside children from Caribbean, Bangladeshi, Pakistani, Somali and Yemeni families. It was, she says, 'what it first meant to me to be Welsh'. But that changed: as she grew older she was exposed to the gamut of racism from the 'polite yet no less othering... Where do you come from?' to a physical attack, which the police were informed about but took no action. Marvin Thompson, born in London, now living in south Wales, winner of the Poetry Society's National Poetry Competition, another radicalised, angry contributor, uses his poems 'as shields against the spears of racism hurled at the Black body and the Black mind'.

Charlotte Williams's contribution establishes how we stand currently in the education system: only 3 percent of teachers in schools are from ethnic minority groups – a paltry figure highlighting the monocultural bias that has dominated teaching and learning down to the present. She notes that a petition to the Welsh government asking for Black history to be made a mandatory part of the new Curriculum for Wales collected more than 34,000 signatures. It produced a result. A ministerial working group subsequently advised that schools should give due attention to the histories and contributions of Black, Asian and ethnic minority groups across the curriculum. The desired outcome will not be achieved overnight, but it is a vital right start.

And in the poet Hanan Issa we have a glimpse of the goal of the racial and religious equality that would make the world of Wales a better place. A Muslim whose Welsh mother was a convert to the faith, she writes of an earlier convert, Lord Henry Stanley, 1827–1903 *(not* the Stanley who met Livingstone), whose restoration of an ancient church on Anglesey dedicated to St Patrick incorporates elements of Islamic art work. Traveller, observer, historian, writer, Lord Stanley is a model for her own thoughtful, compassionate response to society's ills. She writes of her Iraqi heritage originating in the Mesopotamian marshes and of 'one loyalty and another [flowing] as easily for me as one body of water running into another... A stream and a river, a Muslim and a Welshwoman', and of the encouragement to those of her faith to 'honour trees' and 'plant seeds even if facing the end of the world'. In succession to Ifor ap Glyn, Gillian Clarke, Gwyn Thomas and Gwyneth Lewis, she has just been appointed National Poet of Wales.

Guaracara

FAWZIA MURADALI KANE

1

Just before the polio epidemic closed the islands down in 1971 and '72, my uncle gave me a morocoy. At least it was alive. The last time he went hunting in the rainforest, he came back with a squirrel's tail, and he couldn't understand why I was so upset. *But look how fluffy*, he said. It wasn't. It was threadbare. Pictures of squirrels in Foreign show them bushy and red. Trini squirrels maaga for so, despite their greediness. Years later, I learnt that hunters were paid a bounty per squirrel, as they loved to chew through the hard skin of coffee and cocoa pods for the sweet beans inside.

2

Guaracara river was a black thing, iridescent, slow moving, sticky with waste from the refinery as it poured its pollution into the Gulf of Paria. The banks were slick with oil. The trees were stick-thin, stained outlines of a cartoon hell. Nothing could grow there.

3

There used to be a railway line, snaking behind these back streets of Marabella. It ran a few hundred yards to the north of our house, past the empty plots stretching under the huge spread of the ancient samaan tree behind us, and over a Bailey bridge spanning the river. I remember the freight trains, trundling past with wagons heavy with fresh-cut cane stalks. A sickly molasses scent wafted well after they passed. My brother warned us off going too close. He said once a boy tried to grab a cane stalk while the train was moving, and had his arm pulled off.

4

Ramnanan, Ramsamooj, Pariag, Sooknanan, Thackorie: streets to play in, to fetch your brother's cricket balls when he hit a six, or ride chopper bikes bumping over potholes in the narrow roads. My friend's father built a dollyhouse under their house. Her older sisters were so elegant, wearing makeup while cooking and cleaning in their mini skirts and shindig shoes.

5

After its life as a sugar distribution centre ended, Marabella town became a satellite of Texaco refinery, where workers settled with their families. Shops and workers' eating places stretched along its main road. But when the wind blew down this way, towards the residential districts, the air would stink of sulphur and choked us when we breathed, scratched the back of our throats while we played in the streets. The corrosive rain rotted the galvanise roofs to holes and powdery rust.

6

There was a man who owned land at the street dead-end, near the railway bank. He had set out an orchard years before – mangoes, pomerac, sour cherries. Guavas, downs and pawpaw grew semi-wild along the edges, bird-shit sown. On the Sunday after he sold the land, he poured boiling water over the tree trunks and roots, so no one else could pick the fruit.

7

At seven o'clock, noon, and four o'clock, the whistle went off in the refinery to signal the start and end of the working day. If we heard it while walking to school, we knew we were late. It was a remnant of the war days, an air-raid siren for the refinery, which provided fuel for the motherland of Empire.

8

Every morning the man across the road, who prided himself on being a very knowledgeable and religious man, would line up his six sons in their house, according to their age, and flog them. The smallest first. He would leave the oldest two for last. They were the tallest boys in these parts, known for being strong as bullocks but not worth schooling. If my uncle visited us during these times, he would peer through our window and shout *daily blessing bwai!* and the man would stop. Two years later the religious man emigrated with his family to Foreign. The youngest boy married a delicate young woman, and kept her captive for months. Her uncle somehow managed to retrieve her, and brought her back home.

9

The train system was broken up and buses took over the roads. The rails and wood sleepers remained. We played in the gaps between overgrown razor grass. My oldest sister would carry me for walks, cradled on her shoulder, pretending she was grown up. Once she tripped on a stone. I was thrown over the rails, landed on my face on the gravel bank. I didn't cry. My mother told me how she slapped my sister after seeing my bloodied face. I don't remember this, but my nose is crooked.

10

Once a centipede stung a boy. His leg swelled like a purple boot. *Santipee nearly kill 'im!* His family went to live in Canada. He died driving on the icy roads there, many decades later.

11

Over the years, squatters settled over the rusting rails, along the unclaimed state land. They built dwellings from discarded timber, cardboard and recycled plywood – materials easy to dismantle and reassemble quickly, should the government bulldozers turn up unannounced. In time, the area became known as the Line.

12

My sister would complain that I never cried. Her friends' toddler siblings liked to bawl. Why wasn't I like them, chubby and noisy? She solved this by locking me in the wardrobe. When I was put in, the dark was so thick you could touch it. She would always relent, open the door, scoop me up with a guilty hug, but sometimes I fainted before. I knew the strange sleep was coming when the whine of the mosquitoes crescendoed to sirens. I remember my sister being beaten by my mother with a length of orange peel, but I cannot say if this was the reason.

13

We would hear the adults whispering about polio in the news. While playing with the other children near the Line, someone said a whole family in the countryside got sick after eating one of the pigs on their farm. Another said it started in Mayaro near the sea, and was travelling to the towns. Travelling. Our word for taking taxis. Flag them down with a pointing finger. Climb onto the seat, join the other passengers. The disease became a live thing. It expanded and billowed dark like the refinery flambeaux, moved with a will of its own.

14

Pappy came home with a truckload of scrap iron and chains. A couple of his refinery welder friends were sitting on the tray. By sunset the swing was finished. My sister and I drive past the old house sometimes. The swing is still there, standing in the immaculate garden of the house's new owners.

15

The time came when we couldn't walk into each other's houses or play in the street. That epidemic year the Common Entrance exam was delayed. The newspapers began to publish mock exam questions, while the School Teachers Association tried to give lessons over the radio. Pappy went to school to collect my homework. I could tell he was enjoying this more than me. An assignment was to guess the number of grass leaves on our lawn. He went into his shed and came back with a ball of string, a mallet and wooden pegs. My heart sank. He pegged out the small front garden, tying the string into foot-wide grids. Mister Morocoy kept me company, eating the scuffed patches of lawn under the swing, while I counted. Pappy handed in the pages of methodology, calculations and conclusion. Mrs. Murchie called me on the phone. She laughed, *you were supposed to guess, that's all.*

16

I remember when the river caught fire. The water was already thickened with oil-sludge. Someone lit their rubbish and the wind threw sparks onto the water's surface. We stood in our street a half-mile away, and watched the bonfire's flames grow taller than the houses. It burnt through the night, despite the drizzle. The glow moved slowly, followed the river's slackened flow to the sea, catching the crude covered trees along the banks, to bring death to the already dead.

17

We queued up with the Marabella Line children for the vaccination in a temporarily opened school: dosed with a sugar cube on a plastic spoon, smothered in pink syrup. A girl behind me bawled non-stop. Pappy was silent on the way home. Later that day he brought us ice cream and fried wontons. I put Mister Morocoy out on the lawn, went inside for ice cream. When I returned, it had disappeared. We searched everywhere, even the guppy-filled drains that lined the road outside. I cried for days.

Running Between Languages

STAV POLEG

My parents discovered socialism when I was eight months old. They moved from Tel Aviv, where I was born, to a kibbutz in the southern desert of Israel, where they would share their belongings and get the same basic salary as everyone else. There, at this utopian community in the heart of the desert, they would leave their baby in a Children's House – a place in which babies and children would spend every night, away from their parents. Perhaps we each have our own starting point, and this version of radical socialism was mine. In the Children's House there was no adult to look after us during the night. But there was a recording machine that could detect cries if they were loud enough, so that a rotating Night Guard would drop by if needed. By the time I was four years old, some children would learn to get out of bed and walk towards the point where the machine was fixed to the wall, stand under it and only then begin to cry – making sure the night guard would detect their cries and come to soothe them. Every morning I made a pact with myself: tonight, I'll walk towards the machine, say that I'm scared, and ask the night guard to come. Every night, I woke up and walked the long corridor until I stood under the machine, a four-year old observing the rickety wooden device, tracing the moon and the way it changed in the window next to it, and never managed to utter a word.

Fast forward to London, Holborn, St Clement's Lane. I'm in my twenties, sitting in a weekly poetry writing class. Outside it is raining heavily and the windows are shaking with such ferocity that I fear they're about to break. We're reading a poem by Seamus Heaney, and I can hardly understand what's going on. My English is so weak, I'm not sure what to make of the title because I don't know what 'Naturalist' is. In the first line, I can recognise the words Year and Heart. Great words to carry a poem, for sure, but not enough to carry my understanding of this line. At the end of the session, I ask the tutor if she could send us the poems we're reading each week in advance. Time, I discover, is all I need in order to wrestle with this difficult language. The tutor replies that unfortunately she won't be able to do this. Time, I'm reminded, is never available when it comes to language, because language happens fast.

Sometimes you have to write in a foreign language even when you're acutely aware that you're writing against all odds. Language always felt difficult for me, and from a very early age I felt that the language I was given quite simply didn't work. So many things happened in my life by the time I turned five, that as a child I felt strongly that – somehow – I had to find a different language. But since there was no other language available for me, I had to invent one. I started to create songs in what today we would describe as gibberish. I would walk for hours in the outskirts of the kibbutz and invent songs in my own meaningless tongue. As a child, there

were too many things that I didn't understand about the world around me, but I think I already sensed a rather crucial thing: that it is always better not to understand something on a literal level than seemingly understand it completely and still not get what's going on.

My parents separated a couple of years after moving to the kibbutz. Turbulent years followed until, when I was five, I moved with my mother and her new boyfriend to another kibbutz, an even more far-left utopian community, a twelve-minute cycle ride from the Sea of Galilee – 'the lowest freshwater lake on earth'. Here, too, I was welcomed into a Children's House and here, too, was a machine designated to detect cries through the nights. But there was also something new: the nights were often punctuated by howling siren alarms coming from the then-perilous border with Jordan. Here, I learned once again that children express fear in at least twenty-four different ways. There were twenty-five of us in this new Children's House. I knew that I was not the only one who was terrified, and yet only two of us were crying in response to the sirens' high-decibel descending and ascending wails.

Back in London, it takes me three months after I arrive to decide that what I really need to do is write poetry. *Poetry* of all things. There is a strong force in me that needs to write – finally, now, I can't wait any longer. And there is also a strange confidence: something tells me that I will be able to wrestle with this difficult language. To a certain extent, I don't mind that I don't understand most of what I read. After all, by now, not understanding is my comfort zone. And perhaps that is one of the reasons I'm drawn to poetry – a space in which one is invited to get lost. I want to dive into English and see what happens. And English is not enough. I want to dive into French and Italian too, I want to swim in languages. Note to self: when you're back home later this evening, check what 'naturalist' means.

English: what a language. All those possibilities of time and space: twelve different tenses and three conditional moods! All those prepositions! At school, I was very weak in English as a foreign language. In fact, I was one of those pupils who weren't able to concentrate at all, on any topic. I was too busy missing my father who steadily faded away until he completely disappeared from my life. I couldn't sit still during lessons, was often thrown out of class and failed at every subject apart from Sport and Art. I wanted to be outdoors – play ball games or go for a run. But later, when my friends became experts at smoking and getting drunk, I knew that if I followed suit, nobody would notice – just as nobody seemed to notice that I spent so many hours out of class. Spending the nights in the Children's House, away from the adult world, we were left to calculate the risks around us on our own. Perhaps some children hoped that if they pushed themselves to the limits, some help would eventually come. I knew without doubt that if I pushed myself any further, I would fall apart. Something had to change. I just didn't know what that something would be.

The arrival of Holden Caulfield, swearing and sweating in outrageously outdated Hebrew in an odd translation from the English, was the most important event that happened to me at fifteen. We had to read *The Catcher in the Rye* for an exam in Literature, and here was a book that I actually managed to read past the first page. It wasn't easy: I remember noting to myself that the translation didn't feel right. The slang and swear words, in particular, felt so old fashioned that it was hard to believe anyone had ever spoken like that. Something told me that the original must be better than the text I was holding in my hands. And yet, miraculously, Salinger managed to shine through this odd mix of dated Hebrew and peculiar swear words, and within a few days *The Catcher in the Rye* became the book that made me realise that reading was an incredible act. For several months, I carried the book in my school bag anywhere I went, the way I carried grief.

I began a habit that would never change: if there was a book I liked, I would hold onto it, I would come back to it again and again. After a few years of holding onto books, I eventually applied for a degree in Comparative Literature. Sitting in the lecture hall at Tel-Aviv University, there was this rarest of feelings: I felt at home. Home, even though it was an odd one: the only available dormitory space was above the university disco hall, which meant studying was forever accompanied by the persistent beat of the bass. Home, even though it was never clear for how long. Some incidents, however brief, seem to anchor themselves in the present tense. This is one of them: towards the end of the first year, while working on an essay on *The Odyssey*, the phone rings. It's my mother. She calls to let me know that they won't be able to pay the rest of the tuition fees. By now she and my stepfather have left the kibbutz only to discover that *you can check-out any time you like but you can never leave*. Or you *can* leave – with nothing. My grandfather, who had sensed this would be an issue one day, had left me a small sum of money to cover the first year of university. But my first year was about to end. I spend the entire night crying to the muffled rhythm of loud disco music. My roommate, an immigrant from France, tells me that in France the tuition fees are free. I'm already working in four different jobs that I hate in order to sustain reading *The Odyssey* through the night. First thing the next morning, I enrol in a French class.

Léa
Elle est pas intérimaire, elle est pas comme ma mère
Elle est passagère, elle est pacifiste
Elle est pas d'accord, elle est passionnée
Elle est pas fut'-fut', oh, elle est pathétique
Elle aime pas tous mes tics...

I love studying French. We have a brilliant teacher, a woman in her thirties who always looks a bit sad and who carries the air of someone who'd actually rather be somewhere else. Perhaps because of this we spend much of the time listening to Louise Attaque. We study the band's 'Léa' in order to practice negation in written versus spoken French. We read Sempé, we watch Alain Resnais and Jaoui-Bacri films. I keep wondering if our teacher realises how brilliant she is. Back at the dormitories, two new students from Ecuador and Panama join our flat. Soon the four of us are wrestling with languages as a way of mapping our opposite directions. The three of them study Hebrew meticulously, treating it as a precious key that will enable them to keep studying and find work. I study French driven by an urgent wish to get away from this country as fast as I can to a different – albeit imaginary – place in which I will no longer need to worry if I can afford to study. We communicate through different levels of broken Hebrew, French and Spanish, while in the background Shakira's 'Dónde Estás Corazón?' Competes with the ever-persistent night-club beats coming from down below.

Dónde Estás Corazón? I didn't make it to France. I landed in Venice as part of a student exchange programme, during which I tried to study Italian while discovering Luna Pop, bursting from every TV station and radio channel: *Cos'è successo, sei scappata / Da una vita che hai vissuto / Da una storia che hai bruciato...* Some cities, however much history they carry, are ever moored in the present. Venice is one of those places: fragile and changing in a matter of hours. A typical day in Venice takes shape like this: in the morning, I study Italian; in the afternoon, I fail to put it into practice. It doesn't take long to learn that any local Venetian I ambush has already lost their last shred of patience for beaming newcomers eager to brush up their skills:

- Vorrei, erm... un caffè e... une, mi scusi, cornetto, erm *un* cornetto, per...
- Espresso? Here you go. Next?

Along with my Catholic Spanish roommate, we embark on the far more gratifying, self-appointed task of researching tiramisu. Soon we are on a mission: to reach and taste each and every variation of *gelato al tiramisù* found on this ancient lagoon; in the process, we learn the city's map by heart. Only the *Acqua Alta* sirens, which become ever more frequent and to which I always react with momentary panic, prevent us from truly accomplishing our work. On weekends, I sometimes accompany my roommate to a rather theatrical Sunday Mass, in which an enthusiastic, rock-star-like priest preaches, hands moving in all directions along with the occasional air-guitar, completing each sentence with *Avete capito? Avete capito?* I like sitting in this space in which I hardly understand a word apart from this refrain. For the first time I let myself grieve for my grandfather who passed away a few months before my arrival in this sea-level city. And it is here, in this space, that I suddenly miss him. *Avete capito?* My grandfather had to learn Italian in a matter of months in order to be able to work with Italian engineers on the Basilica of the Annunciation in Nazareth, a project that was the closest to his heart. All those years, did I bother listening when he told me about the years of working on this, telling me how difficult it was, how meaningful, how exciting to communicate in a different tongue? No, not so much. *Avete capito?* When we step outside, the city is immersed in light fog and rain. There is so much water all around us. No, non lo capisco.

After three months, I packed the fragile city map, the canals and the sirens, the Acqua Altas, the Sunday Masses and a few Natalia Ginzburg books I hoped to manage to read one day, and left with an urgent wish to come back. But a couple of cities and years later, I followed my then boyfriend and left Israel for England rather than the receding dream of Italy or France. And it is in London that I realise I can't wait any longer. I need to write.

For the first few years in London, I can barely communicate in English and find a job as a Hebrew teacher at a reform synagogue. I quickly realise that here too, we speak different tongues. Hebrew is taught like musical notes – the goal is to be able to read it aloud; the meaning of the text is secondary. Following my time in Venice, I have learned to love immersing myself in a language I don't understand, setting my own thoughts free and filling in the gaps. And so, to a degree, I get this. At the synagogue, the pupils' goal is to read aloud a section from the Torah as part of a Bar Mitzvah tradition. Like me, most of them are not coming from observant homes, they don't especially care about the meaning of these religious rituals. But, unlike them, for me Hebrew is a living language, remote from religious texts altogether. While I love the Old Testament as a work of literature, I know very little about religious rituals or texts like the Siddur. Growing up in the kibbutz movement, the religion I was brought up with was Socialism. And this, too, turns out to be rather different from the version I discover in the UK.

I spend the first two years in London wrestling with languages. Teaching a different Hebrew to the one I speak, taking a weekly English class with fellow foreigners who, like me, struggle with the tenses. *The present perfect is not about time, it's about continuity* – the teacher explains – *it's about creating links*, and for the first time I think I actually get something. At night, I spend hours going over a long list of English words, testing myself until I remember what they mean. I find it exciting that English has different words for House and Home, as opposed to the one word that carries both meanings in Hebrew (בַּיִת), French (la maison) or Italian (la casa). I find it frustrating that the verb in 'I miss you' does not convey the absence of someone from your life in a way that illustrates the physical want, as it is in Hebrew: אַתָּה חָסֵר לִי – which is impossible to translate but perhaps roughly means 'you are absent from me'. The French (tu me manques) and Italian (mi manchi) seem to me closer to the Hebrew meaning. Poetry-wise, I find it exhilarating that in English, the adjective comes before, rather than following, the noun – I can already see that this seemingly small technical feature has the most exciting potential for creating surprise and suspense while working on a poem.

Somewhere there is a country in which the hunger for knowledge is met with access to knowledge rather than towering tuition fees. I don't know where this country is. It is not the country I was born in and it is not the country I'm steadily falling in love with. After two years in London, I finally manage to pass the required English

as a Foreign Language test, apply and get accepted for an MA in Creative Writing. Both these achievements feel to me completely incredible. It is not until a few weeks later that I realise how naïve I have been all this time. Even though I manage to get closer to continuing my studies, the obvious, glaring truth was always there – I would never be able to afford the UK's international tuition fees. The small sum of money my grandfather left for my tuition has long gone. I don't know how to describe the months and years of heartbreak that followed this.

I can't go to university in this city so instead I study the city. I study London. The streets and the theatres, the bookshops and libraries, the tube, the bus stops, the galleries, the languages around me. I gradually accept that I'll have to become an autodidact. That I'll have to keep studying, in spite of all my efforts, on my own. And even though this is not my preferred method of learning, it is the only one available to me. To a certain extent, I have no choice, because I rapidly fall in love with the English language: with the multitude of words it contains, with the elasticity of its syntax – how it allows itself to change and move into so many directions and create exciting new forms. English, what a difficult language, what a remarkable language. I keep going to poetry groups during which poetry becomes a form of experimenting. I want to test how the English language works, to stretch its possibilities. Every new, unfamiliar word becomes a word that I test in a poem. The poem, in its turn, turns into a lab in which I check how the word performs in relation to others. Here's an example: I stumble upon a word that I don't know: 'abundance'. I check and test it in a poem: can you say abundance of rain, abundance of nightfall? I start my poem 'After-Party' with the line *Yes, there was the abundance of nightfall* and hope it makes some kind of sense.

There are worse cities than London in which to become an autodidact. When the Institute Français programmes an entire week on the cinema of Agnès Jaoui and Jean-Pierre Bacri, including lectures and seminars with both filmmakers, I learn about the craft of playwriting and filmmaking in the most meaningful way. I'm fascinated by the ways they create tension between action and words, how so often the dialogue in their films and plays is punctuated by the weight of the things that are left unsaid. A few years later, at another event with the same filmmakers, now back in London to promote their latest film, I approach Agnès Jaoui and ask her whether the two of them give workshops for writers while in London. They don't do that, she says, but she is generous enough to share some advice. If you want to progress with your writing, she says while we cross Leicester Square in the rain, if you want to take it seriously, these are the two most important things you should do: first, find a good therapist and begin therapy sessions. Second, don't wait for editors or directors to tell you if what you are working on is good. Be your own editor and director. I was nine months pregnant with my first child when she gave me this advice before dashing away towards Charing Cross Road with her crew. I watched how they disappeared while the square turned into a mix of neon and lightning and smoke. So many things were about to change.

Childhood – that thing that keeps coming back, that close and faraway country, that catalyst of images and sounds. A sandstorm in the desert. A fresh-water lake. Childhood – that unreliable recording machine. Perhaps all new mothers run in opposite directions, back and forth at once. Holding my baby close, I'm pacing in circles all night while simultaneously going for a run in the long corridor that stretches from our rented London flat all the way towards a distant country, a house, a recording device forever anchored to the middle of night. *The present perfect is about continuity, is about creating links.* Sleep deprived and exhausted, I'm tired of links. Holding my baby close for months of restless nights, I find it even harder to comprehend those distant images: the Children's Houses, the long corridors, the siren alarms, the daily ritual of failure – that of walking towards the machine and never managing to speak.

Running between languages, this is what I have learnt: operating in a foreign language is both a constant physical activity and an illusion. You tried to escape language and all you did was get caught in a new one. You tried to create new meanings and you're still trapped in syntax and tenses. Moreover, you now constantly need to catch up with more than one language, because the vernacular changes incredibly fast and the canon shifts directions at equal speed. But one thing I've discovered is this: learning a new language, to a degree, gives you a second chance of childhood, and as a result – a second chance of home. After all, when you acquire a new language you have to learn everything from the very beginning, like a child. You have to learn the concepts of time and space, the days of the week, all the rules around you, how to speak and pronounce each and every word, and so on. And – like a child – you may feel the urge to experiment and play with this language. My language of play, against all odds and my own expectations, has turned out to be English. It has also turned out to be my home.

Looking back, I realise now that even though I grew up in a largely monolingual community, there were many unspoken languages in it. The two kibbutzim I grew up in were largely formed by immigrants and refugees from Poland and the former Czechoslovakia. But no one around me spoke Polish or Czech. Those languages were buried far away in mass graves on dark European lands. Those languages, like the losses and horrors they carried, were not part of my childhood. Although perhaps they were. My grandfather, who lost his mother and father and seven-year-old sister in the Holocaust, refused to talk about any of it with me. But when I asked him once why he'd never told me that my name (which means *Autumn* in Hebrew) means *Lake* or *Pond* in Polish, he looked at me in utter confusion. He was very old by then. He still refused to talk about any of this. But in a rare moment of revelation, he told me

that after the Holocaust, he decided two things: the first one was to forget Polish – the language he was born into and grew up with. The second was to let go of the idea of God.

I've been thinking about these two decisions often. That perhaps, on some level, language and God are always deeply interlinked. That when you reject the language you grew up with, you inevitably doubt your most foundational values and beliefs. My grandfather, who left God behind in the rubble of European ruins, who deliberately forgot Polish, proceeded to immerse himself in six other languages, as if trying to counterweight the loss. My grandfather, who made sure I went to university. How many languages does one need to learn in order to compensate for the loss of one's own mother tongue, of one's own God?

The year before he passed away my grandfather invited me to spend a week with him in Greece. He wanted to see the Acropolis, visit Athens and travel to Delphi. At the time, I was obsessed with *The Odyssey*, and he assumed I'd be delighted to come. But I wasn't sure. He was very frail, and I was anxious that I wouldn't be able to help him if anything went wrong. I lingered on the decision for weeks, but by the time I decided to go he'd found an alternative plan. Perhaps it is fitting that the stories about the oracle of Delphi are stories of a ritual susceptible to misunderstanding. I imagine when pilgrims arrived in the Delphi Temple, the oracle had to interpret their pressing queries, forward them to Apollo, hoping he was not too distracted by the pursuit of mortals as he skimmed through the questions. What Apollo offered as answers was translated back into the oracle tongue and then delivered against a background of hot vapour and fumes rising from the fine, deep fractures of Mount Parnassos.

Sometimes, on sleepless nights, I drift back to the Children's House, to the child walking the long corridor at night, and see it as an image of a pilgrimage; of a daily journey towards the sacred shrine where an open window features a different version of the moon each night, where a machine is fixed to the wall – ready for your urgent pleas and questions. But how hard it is to ask questions as a non-believer; how difficult to ask for anything when you are scared. On those nights, there was no god out of the machine – not even the possibility of misunderstanding, just the absence of sound. But I have learnt to appreciate that during that time, there was another kind of sacred space – found in that long corridor of night, in those hours away from the world of adults – where it was possible to take the time, observe the world around you, and think for yourself. Years later, if you're bound to carry that rickety machine with you wherever you go, you may as well turn it into something else – a backpack, a camera, a sound box to experiment with, and opt for a different kind of pilgrimage, running between languages.

Paula Rego's Studio and her 'Dollies'

ANTHONY RUDOLF

1
Sacred space
– like a bedroom –
entered by few.

We human models
are accessory,
and accessary:

we survive,
a little older,
like the artist.

And the home-made
dollies survive,
they obey

in working hours
the rules of the game.
They keep their secrets.

2
After reading
a few pages
of Daphne du Maurier's

Branwell Brontë,
four miles away
Paula sleeps.

Around midnight
sorcery
rules okay

in the studio:
Paula's dollies
unravel

their inner human,
reveal
their souls,

draw lots
for who does what
and to whom.

3
Free at last
they party,
act out

Kokoschka
beheading
Alma,

his 'silent dolly';
and now,
ambitious like Paula,

the intriguers
put on their style
and perform

Don Giovanni:
'You masqueraders,
why are you calling?'

New Poems

C.K. STEAD

To be continued, perhaps
Horace, Odes I, 11

It's said that to know too much
displeases the gods, so for their sake, my love
stop asking for the end of our story:

no horoscopes, no animal entrails,
forget weather gurus in this time
of storms and climate disasters;

don't think of the waves at their worst
smashing on the rocks at Karekare
but share with me a bottle of Te Mata red.

We'll leave our grapevine and plum tree
to blackbird and thrush and other
untidy feeders, and to the wasps.

Let's talk together not about flashy Love
but the brilliant books and poems it has inspired
and the ones who wrote them –

brainy gossip, and jokes about the times
when there were still flowers to be picked.
Forget tomorrow my love. Just live with me today.

Three Sonnets

On a day late summer in a poem like wine

I ask what it's like out there and she replies
'Gorgeous – "like silk" to quote your lovely poem.'

She must be third or fourth to tell me that –
so I'm known here as a poet, and for a line

that says the water out at the yellow buoy
on a good day feels like silk. For that nice trope

I'm 'famous at Kohi' – but neither my recall
nor my books seem to confirm I wrote it.

Today's one of those rare and windless ones,
the surface all the way to Rangitoto

glassy, while the water that's been tepid
now has a hint of winter, making it feel

indeed like *silk!* – so I catch up with myself
on a day late summer in a poem like wine.

The Death of Orpheus

The death of Orpheus was an unpleasantness
of blood and bone, but the music did not die.

The head that women loved, by women severed
floated downstream to sea, and came to Lesbos.

The hands were gone so it must have been the wind
that played his lyre, and the bruised mouth still sang.

It's said on falling leaves were lyric texts
that looked past winter and remembered well

the wife he lost in the rear vision mirror.
The birds joined in, and streams too, rehearsing

songs the youthful poet made in spring.
If there should be much more of us than shadow

and a name, then yes, in some Elysian valley
Orpheus lives, and sings, and his songs are heard.

Pastoral: Kaiwaka, 1941

Cruelly raped, Mrs Housefly shakes herself,
seems to wash her hands and dry her eyes,

then soldiers on with duties of full summer –
goodies to sample, important eggs to be laid.

She has not read her Shakespeare so doesn't know
of Lear's distress that 'wren and gilded fly

do lecher in my sight'. She has no idea
of her bad press, nor that in one high corner

Sir Spider is composing a web of lies
to capture her or (he can wait) her children.

Out in the yard a boy sits bareback astride
the horse he rides to the gate for mail and meat,

a 9-year-old, doing his 'Bing' or his 'Frank'.
Heifers lift ruffled brows as he sings by.

To 'Amnesia, Muse of Deletions'

Swimming in the dark I call on memory –
　　Rangitoto ahead, and those lights
　　　　of Kohi behind making

a cosy half-circle. Overhead the moon's
　　a waka sailing west to escape
　　　　first light that will put it out.

I'm reaching blind fingers for the yellow buoy
　　and touch it only as the sun does
　　　　dimly through a bank of cloud

remembering Allen's 'Blind Man's Holiday'
　　and our exchange about it. His God
　　　　smelled of laundered linen, mine

(though I didn't have one) of manuka – but
　　a whiff from the Kohi Café of
　　　　breakfast bacon has a hint

of the divine. I'd argued that a poem
　　couldn't do pain and he'd thought that might
　　　　be right but gave it a shot –

his ride by ambulance from Lone Kauri Road
　　through St Luke's, gulping gas and pleading
　　　　'How much longer?' – but learning

the anaesthetic wisdom that erases
　　the searing moment too hot ever
　　　　to be held. Allen is dead

but not his poem, and I remember Lawrence
　　Durrell saying that dying 'makes you
　　　　out of date but brings your chums

to their senses'. Tomorrow, first light swimming
　　I'll ask them both at the yellow buoy
　　　　do the dead forget their friends?

A Proxy for Submission

The Problem with Tastefulness in Contemporary Poetry

ALEX WYLIE

Earlier this year, I happened upon Nathalie Olah's *Steal as Much as You Can: How to Win the Culture Wars in an Age of Austerity* (Repeater Books, 2019). Olah's impassioned and, in its way, necessary book can be epitomised by its statement early on, a statement of its own general view but also one becoming increasingly prevalent, that 'PC culture and aspects of identity politics [have] been used selectively by the liberal media to distract from its own structural biases and inequalities'. Enough said; but it cannot be said enough. Olah's critique in this book is part of a growing body of (leftist) critique of liberal – that is, *neo*liberal – pseudo-progressivism, its cultural-political manifestations and manifestos. Patrolling the round of cultural politics as it does, Olah's critique comes naturally to that most hotly-contested moral high ground of the moment – namely, taste and tastefulness. In the chapter 'The Problem with Tastefulness', Olah makes this operative statement:

> In Britain, in spite of a mild flirtation in previous decades with something more representative, taste has become increasingly judged by its proximity to the middle-class status quo, and by default remains antithetical to anything culturally divergent. It is also a means of ensuring that the status quo is never challenged. ... As a result, we begin to see how taste serves as a proxy for submission; an external indicator of how far an individual is willing to be subsumed by the pervasive modes of power, and play the game of incremental class ascension.

There is certainly a cultural neurosis around taste and tastefulness; but, for me, the problem may go deeper than this, especially in the case of contemporary poetry. What if, I would ask, the 'culturally divergent' and the 'middle-class status quo' are increasingly indistinguishable – if the distasteful itself is that 'proxy for submission', even part of 'the game of incremental class ascension'? Elsewhere in the same chapter, Olah claims that 'in the desperate need to package everything within the narrow parameters of good taste, issues that are infused with anger and rage are mollified and made puny'. But, again: what if 'anger and rage' are now *themselves* within 'the narrow parameters of good taste'? Anger and rage (though I'm not entirely sure of the distinction here) have become implicated with social capital in contemporary culture as in politics, a state of affairs pithily represented, for example, by the current policy in the British civil service of promoting newly-elected trade union representatives to management positions – a mutually enriching cynicism that characterises the current paideia. Rage and etiquette, dissent and officialdom, have become insidiously entangled; the

'narrow parameters of good taste' have, I would claim, absorbed the hitherto 'distasteful'. This cultural-political psychology only works, however, through it not being explicitly acknowledged, by it being precisely a *proxy* for submission, to repeat Olah's phrase: that is, submission at one psychological remove, a confirmation of the 'middle-class status quo' that flatters itself as 'culturally divergent'.

Similarly, much contemporary poetry in the UK is concerned with breaking down the perceived boundaries of various sorts of 'acceptability', in order to achieve a subtler, official acceptability. The problems with this may (or may not, depending on your point of view) begin when you start to consider the necessary socio-political content that this implies: or, more operatively even than that, the socio-political place of content itself. In the age of the 'narcissistic cult of authenticity' (Byung-Chul Han, *The Disappearance of Rituals*), the politically authentic is radically compromised by its exploitation by what Olah calls 'the middle-class status quo'; or we might say power, or capital. To put it another way, 'we' are losing the perception that the authentic is itself constructed, turning a blind eye to the relationship between the natural and the artificial – a relationship at the heart of artistic and social forms, indeed of form per se. 'No Artificial Lifestyle Ideals', a current TV advert for a (very exploitative) craft beer company proclaims, somewhat tellingly. 'Sadly, none of us are really authentic', remarked Asad Haider in a fascinating recent intervention ('PMC Posturing', libcom.org, 19/8/20); or as Thomas Hobbes put it in the preface to *Leviathan* in faraway 1651, 'For what is the heart, but a spring; and the nerves, but so many strings; and the joints, but so many wheels, giving motion to the whole body, such as was intended by the Artificer?' Hobbes, though in most respects the classic conservative liberal, strikes a progressive note, here, in his preface's portrait of the essential constructedness of the 'organic' – or, perhaps, 'authentic' – person, or state.

Though, of course, the personal *is* the political. In her famous, influential essay of 1977, 'Poetry Is Not a Luxury', Audre Lorde characterises 'poetry as the revelation or distillation of experience, not the sterile word play that, too often, the white fathers distorted the word poetry to mean – in order to cover their own desperate wish for imagination without insight'. This was an important corrective, in its own way, of poetry conceived of in *too* formal terms, as well as, of course, its relation to tyranny – but for all this it may fall into the trap of equating language-as-form with 'sterile word play', even with tyranny. The idea of poetry as 'the revelation or distillation of experience' has its own pitfalls and potential misdirections. Any artform can be a 'distillation of experience', and Audre Lorde here, while attacking the 'sterile word play" of European, or English-language, poetry, risks glossing over the importance of language not only in poetry but in political dissent and struggle – and of language itself as an arena of struggle, which surely is more apparent at this time of 'culture war' and self-identification than any other in recent history. Lorde's essay is unapologetically tendentious; but personally I'm not sure anyone would want to venerate "sterile word play". (Presumably one of the "white fathers" Lorde refers to in this way is Shakespeare, whose word-play can certainly at times become sterile – *Loves Labours Lost*, anyone?) It is of course the combination of "distilled experience" and linguistic struggle which creates the revelation of the poem; any diagnosis or definition of poetry which ignores language is necessarily partial. The tendentiousness of Lorde's essay becomes more marked when you read the opening of her poem 'Coal', whose first line takes off from the title:

Is the total black, being spoken
From the earth's inside.
There are many kinds of open.
How a diamond comes into a knot of flame
How a sound comes into a word, coloured
By who pays what for speaking.

This seems to me a poem vividly concerned with how language shapes the individual even as the individual shapes language. The word 'coloured', here, cantilevered at the end of the line, somehow floats above the next despite its huge, threatening weight, before, with a pause of breath as we step over the edge, the sense rushes to be absorbed, though not forgotten, in the next phrase. This a moment of formal revelation which of course carries the power of distilled experience within it – imagination *with* insight. Poetry is definitely not a luxury, as Lorde states in her essay's title: but the essay risks misplacing exactly why this is the case, whereas 'Coal', by contrast, embodies in its momentary, momentous lines a vital poetic sense of 'who pays what for speaking'. 'Some words | Bedevil me', as the poem has it later on: in which 'bedevil' contains, beautifully, exactly the right range of implication.

As such, 'The Problem with Tastefulness' has itself some problems with 'tastefulness', as I see it, especially when considered in relation to contemporary poetry. The objection might come here that I'm transplanting context way beyond the author's intention; I would say, however, that the omission of poetry from Nathalie Olah's critiques of contemporary art and literature in this chapter, and in the book at large, is itself very telling. I think this happens because poetry is a kind of blind spot in these general arguments about distastefulness and 'progressive' literature, about a literature whose role is to 'reflect the extremes of society' – and the contemporary 'renaissance' of poetry in the English language operates in this blind spot. The current mis-coordination of poetry belongs to an ideological – and yes, it *is* ideological – mistrust of the politics of form. As Mary Douglas notes in *Natural Symbols*, as far back as 1970, 'We are witnessing a revolt against formalism, even against form' ('we' here meaning something like 'Western capitalist societies'). Byung-Chul Han, again, offers his diagnosis of this revolt: 'The narcissistic process of internalization develops an aversion to form. Objective forms are avoided in favour of subjective states.' This preference for 'subjective states' is what defines the 'distasteful' tastefulness of contemporary poetry, as a symptom of 'the narcissistic cult of authenticity', which, as Han puts it elsewhere, 'makes us blind to the symbolic force of forms, which exert a substantial influence on emotion and thought'. Since poetry is language considered as form, however loose a definition that necessarily is, it stands to reason that this 'narcissistic cult of authenticity' cannot adequately categorise and use poetry as such; that a political culture that insists on utility, even in its more progressive iterations, cannot understand language considered as form because it cannot categorise it.

Of course, I'm not suggesting that *Steal as Much as You Can* represents this cult of authenticity, but I do think that Olah's inability (or unwillingness?) in the book to consider poetry in 'progressive' terms may be representative of it. 'By reverse,' she continues in 'The Problem of Tastefulness', 'and to expose the shallow veneer of respectability that has been used to conceal policies and ideas that are both cruel and harmful to many people, we require art and culture that is permitted the freedom to flout good taste[,] that at times is allowed to go to extremes, to reflect the extremes that are felt by those communities who are not served by the present system'. A key word here is 'reflect'. There is passive reflection and there is active reflection; the danger here lies in confusing the two. Ironically, a poetry which 'reflect[s] the extremes' of social reality will have the 'shallow veneer' of the mirror – the trompe l'oeil of illusory depth. This is part of the age-old back-and-forth about the social role or use of literature, a debate which centres on a confusion, as I see it, around this idea of reflection, like the famous one in Stendhal's *The Red and the Black*:

Ah, Sir, a novel is a mirror carried along a high road. At one moment it reflects to your vision the azure skies, at another the mire of puddles at your feet. And the man [*sic*] who carries the mirror in his pack will be accused by you of being immoral! His mirror reflects the mire, and you blame the mirror! Blame rather the high road on which the puddle lies and still more the inspector of roads and highways who lets the water stand there and the puddle form.

This exemplifies the attitude that literature's role is to 'reflect' social reality. But language, history, people, are not like this. Language is never neutral, never simply a polished surface that reflects reality. Neutrality is a kind of pure potential; language is actual. This sort of fantasy of impartiality characterises in our own day the self-flatteries of neoliberal ideology, not least the post-ideological paternalism of the BBC. Olah and Stendhal are focused on content – what is being said, what the reader is being told – and, I think, some contemporary poets are beggared by a similar view of poetry's subordination to fiction (and the social sciences). Poetry, again, being language considered as form, has always (or should always have) a deep investment in how speech shapes and has shaped the writer, even as the writer shapes the poem. The poet is not the same person when they finish the poem as they were when they started it; neither (hopefully) is the reader. The poet is not innocent; neither is the reader. Words bedevil us. Active recognition of this demands those 'reflective Powers of the mind' of which Samuel Taylor Coleridge, one of the most important reflectors on reflection in the English language, wrote in the *Notebooks* – a Power which is 'self-witnessing, and self-effected', rather than 'permitted'.

The liberal-left co-ordinates of Olah's injunction here lie in the semantics of her extolling of an art against good taste – it must be 'permitted the freedom', it must be 'allowed to go to extremes'. Here we are still within the narrow parameters of 'approved' art, despite the thrust of what Olah says throughout this chapter, and the book – and this is no trivial linguistic quibble. 'As society shifts, so the values we've taken as definitive need to be reassessed to ensure they reflect who we all are as people, and what we want to achieve as a society. To do so, art must be permitted the freedom to reflect the worst sides of ourselves.'. This Stendhalian art of passive reflection will always be a 'permitted' art. And, again, this makes the basic assumption that society always precedes art: art in this view is 'permitted the freedom' to do what it needs to do to benefit society: a strange kind of freedom since, if we were talking about an individual 'permitted the freedom' to serve the person granting the freedom, we would be talking about servitude. Poetry considered in terms of its reflective content is indeed a poetry engaged in wage labour, free to express itself in the terms of its employers – occasionally 'permitted the freedom' to go home at 4p.m. on a Friday (or to appear on Radio 4 on a Thursday). Art that is 'permitted' will always be within 'the narrow parameters of good taste', no matter how much it 'reflect[s] the extremes' of its society.

Art, literature, poetry, should not reflect, but embody. Embodiment requires a deep perception of the forms that create art, society, and the individual alike, the hidden (and half-hidden) structures lurking within that sacred space of neoliberal content, the so-called 'individual voice' (which is really just one of the auras of consumerism). If contemporary poetry has 'connived at its own irrelevance', as Jeremy Paxman notoriously claimed on *Newsnight* in 2014, then it is for these cultural-political reasons. There is a contemporary aversion to form and formalism that is itself cultural-political – not unrelated to the postmodern horror at the likes of Hegel and Marx – and which is the source of contemporary poetry's 'irrelevance'. In Paxman's terms, poetry can only become 'relevant' by being divested of what actually makes it truly relevant as an artform, namely its (de)construction of what the 'relevance' of the age actually constitutes and is constituted by. An art that longs for immediate relevance longs for approval of various kinds; an art that longs to be to people's taste tends toward the tasteful – though in the current moment, this sense of taste is subject to the usual ideological self-evasions. A poetry which really does resist the 'pervasive modes of power' is one which absorbs and remakes them through its *own* 'self-witnessing, and self-effected' modes of power, refracting, rather than reflecting, the voices, the idioms, the languages that construct us, and that we construct. Or perhaps Hobbes's preface can serve as epilogue here: 'But there is another saying not of late understood, by which they might learn truly to read one another, if they would take the pains; and that is, Nosce teipsum, Read thyself.'

From the Archive

from *PNR* 257, Volume 47 Number 3, 2021

Orchard

Then there was peace in Wexford, some cars
In the distance the sole night noise.
We were moving slyly towards the trees,
Soundlessly shifting among brambles and briars.

Windows fading out into the dark
Belonged to unimagined space.
Nothing grew easily here, the gnarled
Half tended back of somewhere. When

Branches gave, she must have heard and stirred.
The wet night earth smelled rank and sour.
Sound of a lock pulled back, a key being turned.
Followed by stillness now the years have gone.

Colm Tóibín

more available at www.pnreview.co.uk

'The Critic as Cleaning Lady' and other poems

MILES BURROWS

Under the Bed

Is there some other poem, finer, not quite written,
In the shorter volume, lurking in its margins?
Handwritten, or bleeding, rainsoaked, in purple ink?
Or on some India paper, vellum bound, invisible,
Sent from some dying major in the Himalayas
Scanning the stillness of the leaves across the valley
For signs of enemy movement? Movement of any kind?
Why always call the same unearthly batman,
Barefoot, spilling Japanese heads from a burlap sack?
On a Sunday evening like this one, full of shredded wheat,
Is it not time to brave an early cheroot?
Take off your shirt now, hero, and start ironing
The only shirt that God has given you
Or will you look for shirts in azure and purple
Belonging to the dead in their flames,
To seraphs in their aertex pantaloons?

How to Write a Poem

First: what is the aim of your poem?
What is it for? For whom? Why?
Who will gain from it?
Is poetry the thing? Consider alternatives.
Do you want to write it yourself?
Consider getting someone to write it,
Or reclaiming a disused poem you may have found.
Many successful poems have been written in this way.
If you wish to go ahead and write it yourself from scratch
Think: What kind of poet are you?
Are you the kind who is found in a cave hanging upside down in a jar?
Or do you prefer writing after supper and whisky
With a cat on your knee, listening to Bruckner?
Think again: what is the purpose?
A poem should appear tailor made
And visibly hand stitched by a recognised English tailor
From good material after several fittings
At a certain period and season of the year.
All too many appear like off the peg research papers,
Perfunctory, fashion-tweaked,
In recurrent anxiety about tenure, jaunty
As an ageing don in salmon pink trousers,
A ring in one ear.

The Critic as Cleaning Lady

If poetry is a rash, it calls for a diagnosis.
You take your temperature. The doctor says it's viral.
And while it would be too much to claim
That without diagnosis there can be no disease
Yet the label holds our interest more than the rash
And lends distinction if in German.
The critic as Cleaning Lady, with his smiles and buckets
Enters stage left with a clatter of apparatus
And a lugubrious private agenda. She's good for a chat.
And dominates the stage. She can't help it.
It is the nature of her work, her joy, her glory,
To hoover underneath just where the poet is sitting,
So he has to move. And if the poet is dead already
She chatters on while continuing to dust him
And suddenly stops to give a delayed theatrical scream
Which the audience enjoys because they knew this would happen.

Mr W. H.

JEFFREY MEYERS

W.H. Auden, *Poems. Volume I, 1927–1939* and *Volume II, 1940–1973*, ed. Edward Mendelson (Princeton), £48 each

In his Preface to *Collected Poetry* (1945) W.H. Auden observed that an author's work falls into four classes. First, 'the pure rubbish'; second, the good ideas that came to nothing; third, the pieces that lack importance; fourth, 'those poems for which he is honestly grateful'. Despite his impressive success, he was always severely critical of his poetry. Never quite satisfied, he frequently revised after publication. This superb 1,946-page edition confirms that Auden looked far out and in deep. His technical skill, ideas, intelligence and wit made him the greatest English-language poet born in the twentieth century.

Edward Mendelson writes that '[t]his edition contains all the poems that Auden published in books, magazines and newspapers; also the few poems that he submitted for publication but which for various reasons did not appear; and the few poems that he sent to friends as what he called "posthumous" poems for publication after his death'. During Mendelson's painstaking and perfect work of several decades, he even tracked down privately owned manuscripts for the detailed textual notes on Auden's dates and places of composition, publication history and extensive revisions. To make this edition complete, he acknowledges the inclusion of poems from Katherine Bucknell's edition of *Juvenilia* (1994, expanded in 2003). The 570 pages of textual notes are mainly of interest to scholars. The only error I noticed is that Dale Wasserman was the writer, not the producer, of *Man of La Mancha* (II.1091).

Since (by Auden's request) there is no edition of his letters, his quoted correspondence with friends and editors, and comments on his own work, are valuable. In June 1927, for example, T.S. Eliot at Faber rejected Auden's first book and offered some slight encouragement: 'I do not feel that any of the enclosed is quite right, but I should be interested to follow your work.' In 1932 Auden wrote of his opaque *The Orators*: 'I am very dissatisfied with this book. The conception was alright but I didn't take enough trouble over it, and the result is far too obscure and equivocal.' That year Eliot, who'd inserted Sanskrit words into *The Waste Land*, told Auden 'there is no need to apologize for obscurity'. In 1936, when Cape had arranged to finance Auden's trip to Iceland for a travel book, Eliot – eager to retain his valuable author – vigorously protested and Auden got Cape to release him. In 1950 Auden peremptorily criticized the binding of *Nones*: '*What* is that patent forgery of my signature doing on the front? I trust it is not intentional. It must disappear.' He claimed he didn't like to comment on his own poems, but often explained them in long letters.

Auden's brilliant opening lines seduced readers into his poems. Sleeping under the sky in summer, he saw one of the brightest stars: 'Out on the lawn I lie in bed, / Vega conspicuous overhead.' Sensitive to animal suffering, he wrote the mournful lines: 'Our hunting fathers told the story / Of the sadness of the creatures.' He commanded attention with the imperative: 'Look, stranger, on this island now.' The revolution of the planet produced unusual sensations in body and in bed: 'The earth turns over, our side feels the cold.' During a tremulous geological convulsion 'Night covers up the rigid land / And ocean's quaking moor.'' One of his best passages appears in 'The Fall of Rome': 'Altogether elsewhere, vast / Herds of reindeer move across / Miles and miles of golden moss, / Silently and very fast.' In this vast Arctic space the mass of reindeer, despite their great numbers, are silenced by the soft cushion beneath their hooves. This cinematic image resembles the scene where precious sables are set free and race across the snow at the end of the film *Gorky Park*.

Auden's early love lyrics, his aesthetic defense against emotional pain, are ironic yet surprisingly tender: 'Sleep on beside me though I wake for you: / Stretch not your hands towards your harm and me, / Lest, waking, you should feel the need I do / To offer love's preposterous guarantee.' In an aubade, when the lovers are threatened by the ravages of time, disease and death, they seize (with a pun on 'lie') the moment of sensual bliss: 'Lay your sleeping head, my love / Human on my faithless arm; / Time and fevers burn away / Individual beauty from / Thoughtful children, and the grave / Proves the child ephemeral: / But in my arms till break of day / Let the living creature lie, / Mortal, guilty, but to me / The entirely beautiful.' In another poem he slyly undermines the romantic idealism: 'Unhappy he who after it is sucked.'

The ballad 'As I Walked Out One Evening' portrays the inevitable delusions of love. Auden invokes the 'orient and immortal wheat' of Thomas Traherne; mentions the lovers, with nowhere else to go, seeking intimacy under a railway arch; and evokes a series of impossible promises to sustain their love. Suddenly the hopeful mood changes as menacing Time coughs like a doomed tubercular 'when you would kiss'. The image of 'appalling snow' both covers the pale valley and suggests the pall of death. In a rhetorical series 'O plunge', 'O look' and 'O stand', Auden twists Matthew 22:39 into 'You shall love your crooked neighbour / With all your crooked heart'. In the end life flows on but the warning has been sounded. There's no resolution between the lovers' idealism and the forces that will destroy them.

Auden said of *Letters from Iceland*, 'I've never enjoyed writing anything so much before', and composed the 'Letter to Lord Byron' in a seven-line variant of the *ottava rima* of *Don Juan*. Subtly adopting Nietzsche's idea that disease inspires art and echoing Gray's 'Elegy', he states, 'That many a flawless lyric may be due / Not to a lover's broken heart, but 'flu.' He originally wanted to be a mining engineer and, in a witty reversal of expectations, praises the ugly landscape of the industrial Midlands: 'Tramlines and slagheaps, pieces of machinery, / That was, and still is, my ideal scenery.'

D.H. Lawrence condemned this scenery and the exploitation of miners in *Sons and Lovers*. But in Auden's Foreword to *The Orators*, he listed Lawrence's *Fantasia of the Unconscious*, and the 'sinister' novels of power, *Kangaroo* and *The Plumed Serpent*, as important literary influences. Lawrence tore off the mask of Victorian hypocrisy and revealed the sexual 'sensations hidden by shame'. Though Auden was certainly peripatetic and prolific, he asserted, 'I am no Lawrence who, on his arrival, / Sat down and typed out all he had to say.'

Auden's hero T.E. Lawrence appears briefly under his military pseudonym: 'Shaw of the Air Force said that happiness / Comes in absorption: he was right.' Lawrence, a war hero who also inspired the hero Ransom in *The Ascent of F-6*, died in a motorcycle crash in 1935. Auden declares that his violent, even suicidal death, like his life, was also 'right', even though Lawrence was only forty-six. But at least he avoided a degrading deterioration: 'Death like his is right and splendid; / That is how life should be ended! / He cannot calculate nor dread / The mortifying in the bed, / Powers wasting day by day / While the courage ebbs away.'

Many of Auden's couplets in *Letters to Iceland* are impressively compact. He defiantly demotes an overrated artist in favour of two skilled draftsmen: 'All Cézanne's apples I would give away / For one small Goya or a Daumier.' He skewers the crankish concept of his sometime mentor Georg Groddeck by remarking: 'I can't think what my It had on Its mind, / To give me flat feet and a big behind.' Wyndham Lewis's vitriolic personality, reactionary politics and intellectual isolation are all compressed in an explosive metaphor: 'There's Wyndham Lewis fuming out of sight, / That lonely old volcano of the Right.' (In another poem Auden explains in a single line why Matthew Arnold mysteriously abandoned poetry: 'And thrust his gift in prison till it died.') The nineteen-page annotations of Auden and Louis MacNeice's 'Last Will and Testament' are excellent and most welcome.

In the mid-to-late 1930s Auden moved restlessly from Iceland to Spain, China and, in January 1939, to America, and used poetry to comment on politics and war. In 'Spain' he expresses the need for personal commitment and risk to defend the Spanish Republic against the fascist military rebellion: 'I am your choice, your decision: yes, I am Spain.' He famously concludes that the victors always have the last word: 'History to the defeated / May say Alas but cannot help or pardon.' Mendelson slightly misquotes 'Inside the Whale' by George Orwell, who'd been wounded fighting in Spain and fiercely attacked Auden's phrase 'the necessary murder': 'It could only be written by a person [not by 'someone'] to whom murder is at most a <u>word</u> [should be in italics].' Alluding to Auden's noncombatant status, Orwell adds, 'Mr Auden's brand of amoralism is only possible if you are the kind of person who is always somewhere else when the trigger is pulled.' Wounded by Orwell's comment, Auden changed 'necessary murder' to 'fact of murder', cut 'Spain' out of his *Collected Poems* and refused all requests to reprint.

In December 1938, as Europe was hurtling toward war, Auden saw Pieter Brueghel's *Landscape with the Fall of Icarus* (1560) in the art museum in Brussels and wrote 'Musée des Beaux Arts', a masterly use of painting in a poem. In Greek mythology the architect Daedalus fashioned wings and attached them with wax to the shoulders of his son Icarus. Despite warnings, the boy flew too near the sun, which melted the wax, and plunged to his death in the sea. Brueghel portrays a farmer plowing his field, a shepherd tending his sheep, a fisherman angling on the shore, as a galleon with billowing sails passes by. In the distance and across the sea a tiny town and looming mountains are illuminated by the setting sun (too low to melt the wax). The helpless white legs of Icarus, ignored by everyone, disappear into the green water. He symbolizes man's highest aspirations as well as his foolish over-reaching.

Auden announces the theme in the first two words: 'About suffering they were never wrong, / The Old Masters,' and reveals how people like those in the picture remain unaware of their own impending fate. Even during the Crucifixion, 'the dogs go on with their doggy life and the torturer's horse / Scratches its innocent behind on a tree.' Auden notes that in Brueghel's *Icarus* everyone 'turns away / Quite leisurely from the disaster; the plowman may / Have heard the splash, the forsaken cry, / But for him it was not an important failure.' The sailors in the rigging must have seen the boy falling out of the sky but, without stopping to investigate this strange event, 'Had somewhere to get to and sailed calmly on.' Published in 1940, when America was still neutral in the war, Auden's poem alerts readers to the threat to their survival. As Robert Frost wrote in 'Out, Out', 'And they, since they / Were not the one dead, turned to their affairs.'

Auden's 'September 1, 1939' reflects on the historical, political and psychological meaning of the date the Nazis invaded Poland and began the Second World War. He alludes in the powerful first stanza to the brutal invasions of Manchuria, Abyssinia, Spain, Danzig, Czechoslovakia and Austria as well as to the Depression and concentration camps in the catastrophic 1930s: 'I sit in one of the dives / On Fifty-Second Street / Uncertain and afraid / As the clever hopes expire / Of a low dishonest decade: / Waves of anger and fear / Circulate over the bright / And darkened lands of the earth, / Obsessing our private lives; / The unmentionable odour of death / Offends the September night.' The poem had another controversial line that Auden repudiated: 'We must love one another or die.' He insisted, 'It's simply not true that *We must love one another or die*. We must love one another *and* die.' But the cut doesn't help. The whole poem had to be scrapped.'

Auden disliked biography – 'a shilling life will give you all the facts' – but relied heavily on the subject's background when writing his great elegies in *Another Time* (1940). The poem on Herman Melville (1819–91) portrays his life from an adventurous, world-roaming sailor to an office-bound customs inspector in New York, and interprets two of his greatest fictions. Melville's works, according to Auden, dramatically portray the struggle between the good that precariously exists in the world and the insidious evil that is 'unspectacular and always human'. Auden describes Captain Ahab, whose leg has been bitten off by Moby Dick, as 'the maniac hero hunting like a jewel / The rare ambiguous monster that had maimed his sex', and with 'ambiguous' echoes the white whale's ambergris: his 'jewel'. Ishmael, 'the unexplained survivor' who clings to Queequeg's coffin after the whale has wrecked the *Pequod*, lives to tell the tale.

The Christ-like Billy Budd confronts the embodiment of evil in Claggart, the cruel repressed homosexual Master-at-Arms. Claggart taunts and persecutes Billy, who 'wears a stammer like a decoration'. When Billy kills Claggart he cannot explain his fatal blow, and the bud has no chance to blossom into maturity. Billy is hanged by the godlike Captain Vere, who veers toward charity and then shifts back to hanging. Vere's harsh but legally justified 'punishment was human and a form of love'. The poem ends with a reference to Melville's encouraging friendship with the older author Nathaniel Hawthorne, who inspired him as he 'sat down at his desk and wrote a story' – the long unrecognized and posthumously published *Billy Budd*.

Auden's sonnet on the self-destructive Arthur Rimbaud (1854–91) describes the boy-poet's solitude and suffering after he ran away from his unhappy home: 'The nights, the railway-arches, the bad sky, / His horrible companions.' But suffering hurt him into poetry. Auden alludes to Rimbaud's disastrous homosexual liaison with the older poet Paul Verlaine, who shot and wounded him, and to Rimbaud's influential letter about the deliberate derangement of his five senses that would enable the tortured, sacrificial, even insane artist to become a great creator. He published very little in his lifetime, and renounced poetry while still in his teens and at the height of his powers. Then, 'galloping through Africa', Rimbaud became a wretched trader in the wilds of Abyssinia and dreamed of saving enough money to establish a new life back in France. Auden does not mention the grim conclusion of the damned poet's life. His hopes were smashed and he ended up in squalor with an African mistress, a cancerous amputated leg and a crude prosthetic limb that didn't work. His poems, like the powerful beacon of a lighthouse, briefly lit up his landscape and disappeared into the dark until he achieved astonishing posthumous fame.

Auden's sonnet on A.E. Housman (1859–1936) tries to explain the radical fissure between the scholar and poet, between the academic don and the writer who portrayed 'the coarse hanged soldier' with handcuffs on his wrists, a symbol of the persecuted homosexual. Punishing himself for his disappointed love of his London housemate, Housman – 'The leading classic of his generation' (in the UK *Collected Shorter Poems* 'The Latin Scholar of his generation') – wilfully failed his examinations at Oxford University and left in shame without taking a degree. He deliberately chose to spend thirty years editing the dry-as-dust *Astronomica* of Manilius, which had no literary value, and saved up cruel comments to attack his academic rivals. Auden understood the homosexual wound that Housman had carefully cultivated all his life. Alluding to Virgil's *lacrimae rerum* ('the tears of things') in the *Aeneid* and to Housman's compensatory taste for pornography, he observed in a brilliant line that the severely repressed poet 'Kept tears like dirty postcards in a drawer'. Housman treasured his unresolved torments and, like a flash of electric current between two poles, his creative tension sparked both his scholarship and his poetry.

The titles of Auden's finest elegies begin with 'In Memory of...' and pay homage to two men who died in 1939: Ernst Toller and W.B. Yeats. Ernst Toller (1893–1939), the German-Jewish Expressionist playwright and passionate Communist, had led a short-lived Soviet government in Bavaria in 1919 and then spent five years as a political prisoner in Munich. While in prison he wrote *The Swallow Book* (1924) about the birds who'd visited his cell. Auden met and befriended Toller in Sintra, Portugal, in 1936 and addresses him in the elegy as 'Dear Ernst'. Like Rimbaud and Housman, Toller was a tormented man. Depressed by the failure of his plays in America, the desperate lack of money, the spread of Nazism in Europe, the news that his brother and sister had been sent to a concentration camp, the defeat of the Loyalists in Spain and the threat of another world war, he hanged himself with the cord of his bathrobe in a New York hotel room.

Auden's most personal and heartfelt elegy tries to account for the tragic suicide of the 'egotistical and brave' Toller. He asks if it were childhood trauma or political failure and imprisonment that fatally injured him and made death seem 'friendly'. His sacrifice was both a noble example and a fierce warning to the young. But Auden, unable to find a convincing psychological or political explanation of his death, wonders if Toller had been driven by unknown forces. In powerful closing triplets, he continues to lament the death of his friend: 'We are lived by powers we pretend to understand: / They arrange our loves; it is they who direct at the end / The enemy bullet, the sickness, even our hand. / It is their to-morrow hangs over the earth of the living / And all that we wish for our friends: but existence is believing / We know for whom we mourn and who is grieving.'

'In Memory of W.B. Yeats' (1865–1939), Auden's most virtuoso performance, employs three different metrical and stanzaic forms to imitate three poems by Yeats. He died in 'the dead of winter' and the poem opens in a hyperborean setting: 'The day of his death was a dark cold day'. Auden imagines Yeats's poems as his mourning family who have not been told what happened to him. 'The death of the poet was kept from his poems' and Yeats survives in his work. Auden describes the dying man as a country besieged by revolution. Death slowly conquers his heart and brain and moves to his extremities: 'The provinces of his body revolted, / The squares of his mind were empty, / Silence invaded the suburbs, / The current of his feeling failed: he became his admirers.' As 'The words of a dead man / Are modified in the guts of the living', his readers interpret the meaning of Yeats's work. But his death will have only a minor impact on the populace: 'A few thousand will think of this day / As one thinks of a day when one did something slightly unusual.'

Auden addresses Yeats directly in the second section, commenting on his character and relations with his patron Lady Gregory, his 'silly' mysticism, spiritualism and fascist sympathies. In 'The Man and the Echo' Yeats had guiltily asked about the effect his fiery nationalistic play *Cathleen ni Houlihan* had had on the Irish rebellion, 'Did that play of mine send out / Certain men the English shot?' Auden challenges this statement and absolves Yeats by dubiously asserting, 'poetry makes nothing happen'.

The third and most formal section, echoing the form of Yeats's 'Easter, 1916', is based on his epitaph on the Irish patriot Jonathan Swift, which in turn was based on Swift's Latin *saeva indignatio* epitaph on himself: 'Swift has sailed into his rest; / Savage indignation there / Cannot lacerate his breast. / Imitate him if you dare / World-besotted traveller; he / Servèd human liberty.' Auden gives a superb variation: 'Earth, receive an honoured guest; / William Yeats is laid to rest: / Let the Irish vessel lie / Emptied of its poetry.' Time then changes from a destroyer in death to a preserver in the afterlife, and pardons reactionary writers like Kipling, Paul Claudel and Yeats for writing well. Taking up the life-giving water imagery in section two – 'it flows south / From ranches of isolation' – Auden alludes to Christ cursing the fig tree in Matthew 21:19, and suggests that the poet can transform evil into beauty and reveal how to survive in a cruel world. Art reveals a way out of this trap: 'With the farming of a verse / Make a vineyard of the curse, / Sing of human unsuccess / In a rapture of distress;... In the prison of his days / Teach the free man how to praise.'

Two major poems, which appeared in *Nones* (1951) and in *Homage to Clio* (1960), contrast the landscapes and cultures of England and Italy. 'In Praise of Limestone' celebrates the malleable and anthropomorphic rocks of his native Yorkshire. The opposite of durable granite and marble, limestone is as soft, secret and companionable as the human body. Auden concludes this long-lined ramble through the countryside by connecting it to sound and sight and personal affection: 'when I try to imagine a faultless love / Or the life to come, what I hear is the murmur / Of underground streams, what I see is a limestone landscape.' Auden explained that this 'rock creates the only human landscape, i.e. where politics, art, etc. remain on a modest ungrandiose scale'.

Auden owned a summer house on the island of Ischia. When he left Italy for a village in Austria he contrasted the two cultures in 'Good-bye to the Mezzogiorno': the carefree character of the South to the austere temperament of the North. He defines the Northern qualities as Protestant, gothic, solitary, introspective, guilty, contentious, cloudy, pallid, beer-drinking and joyless. The hedonistic South offers a plenitude of pleasures: Catholic, Baroque, operas, blue skies, sunshine, vineyards, luscious food, gesticulations, *amore* and *la bella figura* of stylish women as well as crowds and noise. And yet, with all the sensual delights, he fears he will degenerate if he prolongs expatriate life: 'To "go southern", we spoil in no time, we grow / Flabby, dingily lecherous.' Despite the aesthetic joys of Bernini, Bellini and Verga, Auden must reluctantly leave: 'though one cannot always / Remember exactly why one has been happy, / There is no forgetting that one was.'

At the end of the sophisticated romantic comedy *Four Weddings and a Funeral* (1994), a Scotsman reads Auden's little-known 'Funeral Blues' at the interment of his male lover. The poignant poem expresses his desolate mourning: 'Stop all the clocks, cut off the telephone, / Prevent the dog from barking with a juicy bone, / Silence the pianos and with muffled drum / Bring out the coffin, let the mourners come... The stars are not wanted now; put out every one, / Pack up the moon and dismantle the sun, / Pour away the ocean and sweep up the wood; / For nothing now can ever come to any good.' It's amazing that Auden's colloquial poem can be so effective in a contemporary film.

Auden can be magically conversational, charming and sophisticated, vivid, lyrical and amusing. A master of rhyme and metre, he has a brilliant range of allusions and important ideas, wisdom and moral force. Aware of the threats to the lives and loves of modern man, he explains how we can prepare for that menace: 'In the deserts of the heart / Let the healing fountain start.'

Three Poems

ELI P. MANDEL

hôtel de l'ancien régime

The resort was filling up.
He slept on the top floor,
in a room slightly beyond your means.
Droplets fell on the red cross outside.
I wish you hadn't bought fruit was what he had said.
Everything seemed to come in twos,
which made thinking ungainly,
like the gait of a fat man, and
at the bar the salaryman was saying:
Poetry has been dead in the West since Orpheus,
Dead since it left the underworld.
There was no point in looking up the citation.
You moved the letters around in search of the god's name.
Was it Neutrality? No.
Someone was bearing witness in the courtyard.

a drop of cooling lead

Carew divides creatures into
'things of life, growing and
things of life, feeling'
but for the inanimate world
he has no such subtlety
nor can he give an account of
living things that
neither grow nor feel
the mind in certain casts
falling into a pool
to join the other bullets

sans nuances

1.

You spent your life on a greasy couch.
Beyond the reach of the philosophers.
Where were the gods when you needed them?
Or were they 'always already' here.
A pile of old receipts.
The lyrics in a song you preferred not to understand.
'The truth is I did great things with my life.'

2.
Often you are unfurling a big red carpet.
All this in Swedish about clay objects such as a little pot:
being German or Scandinavian you secretly enjoy it.
The egg wishes it had been consumed raw,
'the rock runs liquid with liquid',
the hook would not hang in the wall.
You really can't say anymore, *The geese at night outside my window.*
Can they have little stones in their hands this winter?
Wherever it stopped being thick,
life washed away like the streak of a snail.

Heritage Psychosis

JOSEPH MINDEN

I was sitting on the sofa, sweating. The electric fire was on. Models of bi-planes swung from the ceiling. A goldfish flinched in its tank.

'It's not someone we can work out who it is, really. No family connection or anything. We just found it at a car boot sale, felt it worth preserving.' Henry looked on eagerly as I turned the brittle pages of the photo album. Page after page of young men, one man present in every photo. That man killed at the Battle of the Somme.

'And this is a Luger P08,' Henry went on. He pushed the album off my lap and handed me a gun. Heavy, black and empty, it absorbed my attention for a moment. I had played with models of guns like this growing up.

'And a fragment of a panel from the body of a Westland Wyvern, found in a ditch next to Fishbourne Roman Villa.'

I laid the Luger on the sofa arm and received the buckled piece of metal, incredibly light in comparison. I bobbed it up and down a couple of times.

'Barely any of them left – most are tinfoil. We luckily managed to get our hands on this when they were digging it up.'

I looked at Henry, hoping I'd be able to meet the need his eyes expressed. 'Amazing,' I managed, with a meaningful extension of the middle vowel. 'Amaaaaazing.'

Henry nodded, satisfied, and turned to pick up what looked like another dusty photo album from the side table. He opened it to reveal foxed, typewritten pages.

'The return of Napoleon from Elba, though a surprise to many,' it began, 'was far from being so to those who, well aware of his restless disposition, his insatiable ambition, and the enthusiastic –'. The sentence was cut off by the end of the page.

'General Cavalié Mercer's Waterloo journal,' explained Henry. 'Original typescript. An object of national – *international* – significance.' He stroked the page.

Strange. When was Waterloo again? I vaguely attempted to compute how the typewriter might have been invented in time to overlap with this soldier's memories, and thought then about the moment, as a child, I'd learned how to make treasure maps, dipping cryptic scrawls in cold tea (a disgusting and inexplicable drink) to fake the look of age.

Elizabeth got onto her knees and slid an old, battered suitcase out from under the sofa. She popped it open. A filthy sack-like thing with a big stain on one side and a large gash spouting horsehair. She looked up silently.

'But this is the pièce de résistance,' she said. 'Have you heard of Manfred von Richthofen?'

I stared.

'The Red Baron. Well, this is the cushion from his plane. He must have sat on this just – countless times. He was sitting on it in his final dogfight, when he was hit, when he fell out of the sky. The stain there's his blood.'

Once this, too, had been put away, I got up to leave. As I made for the door, Henry redirected me into a side room. Just one last thing. He stepped behind a desk covered in clutter and patted a huge bag.

'This is an un-inflated rubber dinghy from a U-Boat. Washed up the Bognor side of Littlehampton. Must have become detached. Absolutely impossible to lift – we had to lever it into the back of our van and slide it in here on a pallet.'

There it stood. When had it washed up, I wondered weakly. Then or now? Moving past me towards the coat rack, Henry turned and pointed back to the corner of the room. A longsword stood upright, its tip sheathed in a wooden stand that resembled the stump of a tree trunk. There was a pink jewel in the pommel.

*

Between August 2014 and August 2018, the four years of the First World War centenary commemorations, I was working as a Development Officer for the National Lottery Heritage Fund (NLHF). My job was to help organisations and individuals apply for money to 'make a lasting difference for heritage, people and communities'. Consequently, I had a lot of encounters like this.

I never loved the job. I always felt like an imposter. I knew little about history, nothing at all about project management and lacked experience in any branch of the heritage industry – curation, education, fundraising, marketing and so on. I hadn't even known, prior to starting, that a thing called 'the heritage industry' existed. I had been drawn to the sector on account of a childish unwillingness to confront the tedium and sharp edges of adult life.

Growing up in Cambridge, I'd enjoyed trips to the Fitzwilliam Museum, to Wicken Fen nature reserve and to Wimpole Hall. I associated these places with the softness of holidays, with my parents' time off, with the comfort of being both minded and at liberty. This ease had an aura in the present, already a product of the emotional life of memory. Moments – eating a sandwich in the lee of a folly, staring up at a suit of armour – endured as nests made outside the passage of time, beyond the reach of anxiety. And yet, stuck intractably in my past, they became – in Raphael Samuel's words – 'objects of desire', fused to their heritage contents. The prospect of a job that would place me close to this indulgent nostalgia attracted my unserious adult self.

I found I was good at making people like me. I would often end up in living rooms or the ramshackle stores of minuscule museums, drinking a cup of weak tea as enthusiasts tenderly unveiled to me their particular historic passions. The couple who ran Shoreham Fort from a Nissen hut they had erected beside it, entirely against the wishes of Historic England, confessed to me how their shared commitment to the past had shaken them from loveless marriages and into each others' arms. By the time I had cooed, nodded and smiled for an hour, offering some simple advice on filling out the application form, their enthusiasm's reflected glow would have cast me, also, as a benign presence.

On 23 June 2016, the day of the Brexit vote and one week before the anniversary of the battle of the Somme, I was in Sittingbourne, visiting the Historical Research Group Sittingbourne's Heritage Hub. Situated in The Forum shopping centre, in a shop unit leased to them for a peppercorn rent by Tesco, the Hub had been put together with a grant of a few thousand pounds by Richard and Teresa Emmett, an earnest pair of archaeologists-cum-local-historians. We'd finished talking about the plans for their next project and they'd left me alone to see what they'd achieved with the previous NLHF money.

There was a volunteer sitting behind the desk: a neat, elderly man wearing a flannel shirt. I smiled at him as I turned to survey the display. One wall had been done up as the side of a trench, with fake earth, leaf netting and pallets to imitate duckboard. There were several caps, helmets, lanterns and tins evocatively placed on ledges within the structure. In front of this, there was an iPad on a stand, containing the Roll of Honour: a database of the names of and, where possible, photos and further information relating to 3,000 local men who had fallen in the First World War.

I scrolled through some of the names and stories desultorily and then turned to the bookstand, examining a handful of works of local history put out by The Faversham Society. I smiled again at the volunteer as I walked towards the door. 'That's the trouble with your generation,' he said, suddenly, catching my eye and leaning forward. 'You have no idea what it means to care about your country.' My smile died, but I didn't know what to say.

*

Wilfred Bion, who would go on to become a celebrated psychoanalyst, served as a tank commander in the First World War. I discovered his memoir of this experience, *The Long Week-End*, in a second-hand bookshop in Rochester after a meeting with Medway Council; I began to read it on work journeys out of London, along the north coast of Kent or down into Hampshire. As far as I could tell, he didn't care too much about his country, either. Nor did he feel like anything other than an imposter when he found himself, at nineteen, in charge of a tank at Ypres.

On paper, Bion covered himself in glory during the war, receiving the Distinguished Service Order for his actions at Cambrai. But his accounts of his experiences are devastating, not least in its understated disgust for the 'public school culture' that could 'believe in the fitness of a boy of nineteen to officer troops in battle.' Survival, as he presents it, is a succession of slapstick catastrophes exhibiting grotesque and undignified good fortune, along with the squalor of complete incompetence in a crisis: Bion is quite prepared to describe himself as 'typical of the damned fools that were made

combatant officers'.

His tone is matter-of-fact. He is intent on marking in his prose the strange banality with which reality strikes the mind. The extreme experiences of the war only serve to highlight this phenomenon, which emerges as a fundamental psychological insight. Regardless of the level of horror, events register bluntly, without fanfare or drama. Workmanlike sense receives them. Recounting his response when his runner, Sweeting, abruptly asks him why he has become unable to cough, Bion writes: 'What a question! What a time... I looked at his chest. His tunic was torn. No, it was not his tunic; the left side of his chest was missing.'

Pushed to a certain extreme, however, Bion portrays thought simply breaking down. His mind ceases to make sense of the phenomena with which it is enmeshed. Real things become fantasies extended into the corporeal world. The Mark IV tank is less a weapon of war than a metal box into which soldiers climb for obliteration while dreaming of safety. Slithering on Salient mud for the first time, Bion realises how vulnerable and ill-suited to the terrain the tanks actually are, 'no protection more solid than a figment of the imagination'. The tank duly sinks.

Reflecting with astonishment on the fact that no-one predicted this might happen, Bion writes: 'the mud must have seeped into the place where our minds were supposed to be. The army, of which we were part, was mindless.' The mud has both entered the skull and swallowed the mind at large. Nor is the mind singular. The army is characterised as a collective strategy for failing to think, into which individuals are locked in the horror of acting helplessly, without thought.

Looking up from *The Long Week-End* to watch the cranes of Tilbury docks passing in the distance, or Giles Gilbert Scott's Our Lady of the Assumption drift by high up at Northfleet, I wondered what this might mean in the context of succeeding, rather than failing, to think. Potential thoughts would become, by implication, something beyond the capacity of an individual to think alone. They would arise from a collective mentality not mindless but thoughtful, enabling action both for the group and its individual constituents.

*

As I travelled around South East England, my disquiet grew. I could feel something that I did not know. A certain effect was produced by the juxtaposition of one historic thing with another; by the degree to which this dwelling in the domain of heritage continued to activate the warming effects of pleasant, even narcotic, childhood conditioning. The oven at Kentwell Hall, fired up by mock Tudors.

Relatively early on in my time at the NLHF, perhaps around the centenary of the Battle of Loos, I had to make a trip to Portsmouth. On the train down I admired the usual sights: the fringes of Godalming, Guildford cathedral glimpsed on its hill, St Hubert's church – technically 'in' Idsworth but actually in the middle of a field. Maybe more than usual I savoured the landscape, its greenery, the undulations of the South Downs from

Haslemere through Petersfield to Rowlands Castle. I noticed with delight the rear half of a white horse, its head plunged deep into foliage on the edge of a meadow.

By the time the train pulled into Portsmouth Harbour station, it was drizzling and I regretted not bringing my raincoat. The water of the Harbour itself was visible through the slats of the platform as I walked out. Skirting the building site for a new bus station, the Hard Interchange, I approached the wall of Portsmouth Historic Dockyard.

The Dockyard is surely the heritage industry's citadel in that part of southern England – a pioneering redevelopment of a geriatric site into a complex of museums and heritage experiences atmospherically grounded by the hoary ambience. A segment of the still fully functional naval base, it houses, among many other things, the National Museum of the Royal Navy; Nelson's flagship HMS *Victory*; the Victorians' first armour-plated, iron-hulled warship HMS *Warrior*; and the lop-sided remains of Henry VIII's ill-fated pride the *Mary Rose*, dredged up from the Harbour in 1982 in one of the heritage industry's cardinal events. This was my first stop.

'This is absolutely not a military museum,' asserted my chaperone Paul, the operations manager. 'It's about people and the lives of ordinary men.'

On 19 July 1545, with Henry VIII watching from Southsea Castle, the *Mary Rose* had sailed out to meet the massed French fleet in the mouth of Portsmouth Harbour, fired a broadside and, turning, listed hard with the wind and gone down. Its starboard gunports, still smoking when forced under the waterline, had allowed water to rush in. This is one theory, at least.

Caught beneath netting on deck, all but a handful of the five hundred men on board drowned. Paul introduced me to some of them. The cook, Ny Coep, whose enormous cauldron was on display along with an untouched pile of firewood, ready to burn. Two North Africans, one a royal archer with a twisted spine, found trapped beneath a bronze cannon; the other a teenager, 'Henry', his bones bearing the signature of a degenerative condition. At intervals of several minutes, a video recreation of life on board was projected from the exhibition gangways across the skeleton of the ship itself, sitting dessicated in its deep dry dock.

I had been to visit the wreck of the *Mary Rose* while at primary school. In the Nineties, the ship was still being prepared for posterity, continuously sprayed with preservative. It was only visible through little windows, rather like gunports, obscured by droplets of water and mists of condensation. The wateriness was, at least, redolent of the ship's sunken career but it did nothing to mitigate my disappointment, expecting as I had not only an unimpeded view but an entire warship, complete with its whole hull, masts and sails. This was the stately boat that had sailed through my excited imagination on the coach down from Cambridge, the flagship of a transhistorical, nostalgic power already well established in my psyche.

The memory of that trip did not visit me on this occasion, however. Instead, I thought of another school trip, taken when I was a teenager, to the battlefield graveyards of Flanders and the Somme. Strangely deadened by the

ordered, coherent whiteness of Tyne Cot and Serre Road, my muted reaction had turned to horror when we visited Langemark, one of only four cemeteries granted Germany at the close of the First World War. Against the cleanliness, the grief given room, of row after row of headstones whispering, however woundedly, of power and the entitlement to mourn, was set this small, dark plot. Into this plot, ostensibly a wormy and weedy flower bed smaller than the dock in which the *Mary Rose* rested, twenty-five thousand corpses had been shovelled.

The memory of my German grandmother, only recently passed away, set me on the far side of those British enclosures' boundaries and inside the shade cast by Langemark's oaks. It allowed me a first glimpse of the power play of memorialisation. The bodies of the British dead were no less mangled than those of the German. The recovery of any limbs at all was no less challenging. Besides, how much sympathy could one muster for either imperial power. And yet there remained this stunning discrepancy, this unremitting hierarchy, in what had been built to enshrine the bones and scaffold the memory.

For some reason, it was Langemark cemetery that came back to me as I stood with Paul overlooking the wreck of the *Mary Rose*. I imagined the ordinary men of the crew scrabbling in panic as the ship filled with water. I imagined the light rapidly diminishing as the boat sank deeper. I imagined the light vanishing into the darkness of soil. I imagined the 500 bodies turning to 25,000.

*

Wilfred Bion was born in 1897 in Mathura, Uttar Pradesh, during the days of the British Raj, a child of the colonial middle class. The object of his later nostalgia was not England but the 'mixture of tawdry provincialism and Imperial domesticity' of Raj architecture. He was sent to boarding school in England at eight and left school at eighteen to go straight into the Tank Corps, and the destruction of his class and generation's high imperial self-confidence.

Only after surviving the war did he go to university, train as a doctor and become interested in the developing field of psycholanalysis, eventually undertaking a training analysis with Melanie Klein. His early, pioneering work on groups, undertaken in the Forties, was collected in an influential volume, *Experiences in Groups*, in 1961, when he was working at the Tavistock. Shortly after this, in 1962, he published a second book focused on the individual therapeutic encounter, *Learning from Experience*. Many books followed, along with a move to Los Angeles in 1968, where he stayed until two years before his death in 1979.

In *Learning from Experience*, Bion presents ideas concerning the way in which the mind processes experience and establishes contact with reality. Broadly speaking, people can either choose to tolerate frustration in order to develop – thereby learning from their experiences – or to evade it, remaining undisturbed but also arrested. For Bion, an individual may decide to prefer pain in the service of psychological development: thought, working properly, contains the tension that arises, transforming frustration, through attention and encounter, into insight.

Within this theory, Bion hypothesises a kind of psychic quantum called a beta element. Beta elements are the mental impressions of raw data – sense data and emotional experience. In and of themselves, they are not useful to the psyche. They cannot be thought with. For thought to be possible, they need to be in some way metabolised and made available for thinking. The process by which this occurs is mysterious, and Bion designates it with the name alpha function.

The breakdown of alpha function, for whatever reason, leaves the mind with nothing but beta elements. This is the mental state of the psychotic patient, who, according to Bion, cannot think in the developmental way outlined by his theory, and whose waking life takes on the bizarre quality of a dream attempting to happen unsuccessfully. Bion stresses the quasi-materiality of beta elements, as though they are almost literal objects or fragments driven into the psyche and lodged there like splinters; 'the beta-elements are not felt to be phenomena, but things in themselves' he writes. Elsewhere he describes them as 'inanimate objects' and 'undigested facts'.

Because they have not been metabolised in such a way as to be available for thought, the only thing that can be done with them is spit them back out. They are 'suitable for evacuation only'. Bion writes about the arrested nature of patients' attempts to think when only beta elements are available: 'we hear of inanimate objects, and even of places, when we would normally expect to hear of people... live objects are endowed with the qualities of death.' The mind attempting to use beta elements for thought is, in this way, incapable of abstraction. Everything is a concrete image, an object, vividly, intolerably present in the mind.

*

Concrete images. Objects, vividly, intolerably present in the mind. Their continual evacuation. This was how I felt about the thing after thing of the heritage industry, its commodified gobbets of something bad, its imaginary smell of wet tweed, its mist. And these gobbets had the qualities of death, too.

My reverie before the *Mary Rose* was not unusual. In fact, I was entirely used to staring at any heritage object, from any point in the past, only to discover that I wasn't thinking about it at all, but enduring a failed dream about either the First or Second World War, or both. Far from being a weird, associative tic, this turned out to be consistent with the founding logic of the heritage industry; a logic I had stumbled upon several years earlier and which had, back than, seemed counterintuitive.

Before starting at the NHLF, I'd spent a year working as an administrative assistant at the Scott Polar Research Institute's Polar Museum in Cambridge. One day, a man turned up with a box he wanted to sell us. It contained the negatives of photos taken by Captain Robert Falcon Scott himself on the doomed Terra Nova trip, the expedition on which he perished. These were priceless contact plates which, though we had prints of the images, were almost like fingerprints of the ill-fated explorer's eyeballs. We were forced into a mad scramble to try and raise the money to buy them.

If you are ever employed by a heritage organisation suddenly desperate to find cash for an acquisition, the first place you turn is not the NLHF but the more mysterious fund from which it was born: the National Heritage Memorial Fund. This is a 'funder of last resort' which exists to help save priceless historical material for the nation as a 'permanent memorial to those who have given their lives for the UK'. One of its earliest success stories was funding the salvaging and preservation of the *Mary Rose*.

I couldn't understand how any old random stuff – Scott's photographic negatives, for example, or the *Mary Rose*, for that matter – could serve as a memorial for the British war dead simply by being purchased by the British government, so I looked a little deeper. In fact, it was simple. Directly after the Second World War, The National Land Fund, out of which the Memorial Fund (in 1980) and eventually the NLHF (in 1994) would grow, was established as a financial means by which to graft the country's entire historical substance onto the memory of the vanquished.

*

Bion wrote his account of his experiences as a teenager in the First World War at the far end of his life, in the late seventies. It is difficult not to read it both through the lens of his later theories and as their origin story. Reflecting on his thought, the psychoanalysts Joan and Neville Symington suggest that 'the rest of his life was spent trying to assimilate' the War's horrors. The reduction of thought to a paralysed amalgam of fragments, beta elements through which thought cannot move, is fundamental to his picture of the psychic experience of the conflict.

Everywhere in *The Long Week-End*, Bion describes himself as having been 'unable to think' or 'incapable of thought'. At one point he is 'encased in a film insulating [him] from fact'. In other places, the breakdown of thought is delineated as objects replacing each other in the forefront of an overwhelmed perception: 'then I realized, in one of my repeated glances in the direction of trees, that they were not in fact trees but our infantry advancing in a line'.

Facts jostle side by side, undigested and useless as reflection. Where had he learnt about how rain behaves on a summit? 'In Geography class perhaps. No, that was only "jute and flax" growing somewhere or other. Not on Hill 40. Where the hell was Hill 40?' He writes the frozenness of a traumatised mind with astonishing acuity and, while he does not mention beta elements, the abrupt way objects and places disorientate him in succession calls to mind his description of these unassimilable, rigid and disturbing mental phenomena.

Though he writes of the breakdown of thought unforgettably, nowhere is Bion specific about what causes it. At times it seems, self-evidently, to be the horror of war; at others, a kind of ruling class groupthink intolerant of insight; at others still, the mind's attempt to defend itself against unbearable knowledge. This relates sometimes back to feelings of inadequacy: 'My utter ignorance of fighting, as contrasted with the professional soldier's knowledge, was mercifully hidden from me. I could feel it, but I did not know it.' Above all it is this last point – the mind's refusal to grow in the face of unbearable knowledge – that links most strongly with the foundations of Bion's subsequent work, the development of the idea of the beta element and the picture of the mind that can (or cannot) tolerate frustration.

*

The Chancellor of the Exchequer, Hugh Dalton, announced the establishment of the National Land Fund in 1946, in a speech decorated with its very own necklace of heritage fragments. He picks out the 'beauty and history' everywhere in the country; in 'the mist adrift across the moors, the wind on the downs, the deep peace of the woodlands, the wash of the waves against the white, unconquerable cliffs which Hitler never scaled'. He ranges rapturously across the nation's terrain, metamorphosing it, in his final image of the cliffs, into a spectral hint of Dover Castle, the land blending into the historic fabric, the heritage whole impervious to invasion and redemptive of the murdered.

Remembering this speech as I read Bion and travelled from place to object, from object to undigested fact, the idea of the beta element kept returning to my thoughts: not as a perfect analogue but as a persistent analogy. Just as Bion characterised the army as a distributed mind unable to think, I began to see the emergence of heritage as a kind of collective breakdown of thought. The past's discrete items, sustained by the money that sprang from Dalton's Fund and its successors, seemed to crystallise as death masks, the frozen components of a national horror the nation could not really imagine, let alone confront.

For Paul Gilroy, this horror was not just – or even

mainly – to do with the devastation of the wars themselves but rather the crimes of the British Empire, the downfall of which those wars precipitated. Gilroy sees postcolonial melancholia arriving hand in hand with 'the morbidity of heritage'. The triumphalist fetishization of the Second World War serves, in his view, as a way of avoiding any confrontation with the nation's 'hidden, shameful store of imperial horrors'; it serves, too, as a repository of whiteness, a fundamentally racist way of imagining the post-war arrival of Commonwealth citizens in the mother country as a betrayal and the commencement of decline.

By the time the close of the First World War centenary came round in November 2018, which coincided with my departure from the NLHF, I fully agreed with Gilroy. But I also saw something additional at work: the fusion of both World Wars in the production of a kind of heritage psychosis. The trauma of those wars – the loss of men, the loss of the Empire – sat at the root of the heritage culture through which I had travelled, in which I had worked and in which I continued to live. Like a prism, the fused conflicts seemed to refract the whole sweep of the past. Their product, the heritage beta element, the catastrophic psychic shrapnel of English whiteness, constituted the cultural refusal of unbearable knowledge.

When, in 2020, Black Lives Matter protestors tore down the statue of the slaver Edward Colston and threw it into Bristol Harbour, they became an instance of the opposite of Bion's 'mindless' army. Their surge was a moment of collective thought, memory, *succeeding*, driving beyond this refusal and bringing individuals into action. We cannot think the nation's guilt through the interminable maintenance of its historic material, because that very idea is serving an obfuscatory function. Every museum, every heritage centre, every information panel, every plinth – stocked with the debris of a collective psyche stuck in denial.

From the Archive

from *PNR* 247, Volume 45 Number 5, 2019

The Naked Lady

Her bronze body, sculpted by Guillaume, stands sixteen feet high.
She is known – affectionately – as Dirty Gertie.

Her bronze body, sculpted by Guillaume, stands sixteen feet high,
resolute as cars on Regents Park Road speed by.
Many a troubadour in North Circular territory
has courted her with a *cobla esparsa* composed on the fly
over and over, her uncovered sword pierces the sky. [...]

LISA KELLY

more available at www.pnreview.co.uk

Six Poems

PETER SANSOM

Gerard Benson

for Cathy

You were a good age as Dad would say;
like him, mid-eighties, but still young and still
knowing your own quick and open-hearted mind
while your body closed down round you. Those last days
I visited with the proofs of your memoir –
from sent away to Wales to brought nameless back
to gas masks, boy chaperone to a wayward aunt
dancing with her beau (afterwards cake
in a Lyons). ASM, you understudied in rep,
your triumph a walk-on lamplighter
who stole a laugh from nothing, which turned out
the story of your life. You caught the sixties full-on
with the thinking man's crumpet and your own show
at the RFH. Your Barrow Poets' single
topped the Australian charts. Who knew
when you arrived in town with your poet's moll,
your Poems on the Underground and your books
for Penguins, in your natty old-fashioned hat. You strolled
a furled umbrella into our Northern rain
and became its laureate. I loved your work
and like everybody didn't see just how good it is.

Alfie is a Train in the Duck-Duck Park

an express, a word he learnt from me,
the slowest member of the family, so
far away, headlong, by the pond if he
fell or someone took him how would
I get there, but this other train his younger
brother is on time behind me alongside
the playpark in this park which they run
to cross like this stopping only at London
and Sheffield Halloween University
not that Alfie looks like stopping

Larissa and Sienna

In the cavernous old-fashioned back
of a Skoda Superb with its poor visibility,
the girls as they always will be. Lala, calm
behind (inside) a Peppa Pig stickerbook,
a year from being able to read, and Sisi
the big sister looking on, sideways,
just about to comment. The cavern
of a car holds them in their baby seats.
I could cry looking at them. The photo
is my screensaver and looking is
the wrong end of a telescope. I never knew
my grandparents and so I never knew.

What We Did on Our Holiday

In the dark out of the rain with the donkeys
under the pier, Bluebell, Rose and snorting Daisy,
it's a day out from the days, beside the seaside
beside the sea that's actually an estuary
busy with trawlers, containers and the ferry
out of Hull. Then, when the August storm
won't blow over, we gather all our plastic colour
and run to the bright lights and looped blasts
of pop from the penny falls and two pence roulette,
visual candy floss aural e-numbers just
what you want and indoor remote-control boats.
Next stop is the Leaking Boot for fish and chips.

Boarded up and always being done up, this is
Cleethorpes between the bird sanctuary and a big
   wheel
that was old even when the kids were young
and broke down with us rocking at the top.
The Promenade is snakes and ladders and hopscotch
far as ice cream and polystyrene tea as good as it gets.
It brightens sure enough on the land-train back
to the putting. I can still see our shadows
and the chance to explain rainbows in the
skirted round sprinklers. The last half hour
as is traditional is a toy from Beach Bargains
that will last as long as the day.

Pigeons

'Sometimes to someone pigeon fanciers,
Backyard mechanics, rabbit breeders,
Hermit chrysanthemum growers on allotments
And trumpet players in silver prize bands
Are/were/will be great'
    – Stanley Cook

Who'd have thought that doves were pigeons or,
nicer, the other way round. Vermin of the air,
pickers-up in olden times of fag butts in precincts,
scatterers of seeds and followers of ploughs – pigeons,
whose droppings, look, wreck paintwork. That one,
just-landed up there, might have borne the olive branch.
I hope so – with Ararat our roof and the chimney
he looks out from solid ground at last, plain sailing.

Favourite is the pigeon we saw in Pepe's cafe
with the youngest that day when her beautiful
infallible mother announced, 'Look at that penguin.'
A family saying now, 'Look at that penguin.'

Who'd have thought that suddenly it's this year
and here we are with the youngest, the teacher,
by the pigeon cotes at Sky Edge. We stand in the sun
and look, her whole childhood later, at a swirl
of birds in the blue above Park Hill. Then a man
who might be my brother, the one who never
went to school, arrives to let us know all about them.

His dark eyes glitter, seeing them again
in the telling, not the baskets and pantechnicon,
but the start of the flying, when it's not racing
but homing, from as far away as France,
and what he wants to tell us is that moment
that spectacular moment when they're set free
in their hundreds to fill and more than fill the sky.

And equally, here on this one of Sheffield's seven hills,
what he wants to tell us is him, himself, here waiting,
at the far end of the journey. When there she is,
his favourite, unmistakable in all that sky
whether winning or blown anxious days off course

there she suddenly is. And here he always is,
guiding her down with a tin of rattling corn,
not that she needs it, she knows him too, tethered
as she is by instinct or whatever you call it, family.
'Look at that,' he might just as well say, 'Look at that penguin.'

Room

Some way after one of the personas of Fernando Pessoa

The end of the day, I climb up to this room.
They bring a lamp and say goodnight, and I hear
my voice say goodnight, and I forget them.
And for the idea of it make a drink, then settle here
by the window and look out on the street,
houses, a streetlight, and people coming back
from wherever they've been. As if time and people
might let you do it again, do it right, make amends.
I sit with a book but I'm not reading. The day
flows by me, dry river to the sea. Friends
and colleagues, a whole family seems to know me.
Another time a prayer might be said, but nothing's said,
not even, what is it, this. I came here on a whim.
I climbed a ladder to a room and found him.

In a small terraced house and other poems

AMANDA DALTON

In a small terraced house

In a small terraced house
a woman waits through a long night.
She boils a kettle, washes cups,
palms three tangerines
to see if she remembers how to juggle.

The living room's reflected in the yard –
a sideboard hovers on the tiny pond,
her piano juts across the lane.
She's out there too, standing in the hedge,
wonders is it her ghost that waits inside.

Upstairs he lies soaked in pain
but still, the doctor doesn't come.
2am. 4.30. 5.15. She phones again –
a busy night, they say. They're on their way.
She goes upstairs to sit with him

but it's easier to look at a photograph –
the one she'll decide to frame when he dies.
He's on a boat, all smiles, binoculars
around his neck, everything blue
and calm and bright.

That was the day they saw the dolphins
who surfaced, laughing, glided beside them
close enough to touch. A day
of unexpected Highland sun,
a kind of happiness and she wonders –

was it there even then? The start of a mass
in his gut? A stain? Did he feel dis-ease
as it pooled, streamed in his blood? Or was it later,
on Ardnamurchan, driving through pouring rain,
the day he slipped and fell in a storm of magnolia

blossom strewn like confetti on the muddy bank?
The day the deluge blocked the well and she searched
for buckets, found the brook, the stash of bottled
   water,
laughed because this really didn't matter –
then saw how he couldn't cope anymore.

Later she'd walked alone by the sea loch, felt
the slow drip of loss. She wonders was that why
she made a list of everything she saw – to give
to him, to keep something from seeping away

'bladderwort', she wrote,
'white driftwood'
'flowers that might be meadow cranesbill'
'bits of wood'.

She couldn't stop –

'a Tennant's lager can, marsh marigold in clumps, 8
oystercatchers, 14 adult sheep, 9 lambs, a broken rowing
boat, a pair of dark-coloured ducks with 6 young, a crow,
ringed plovers (5), red plastic – might be from a child's
spade, dead crab, a herring gull, sheep's wool, the
remains of a fire, 4 black-headed gulls, a plastic shoe
(green), campion, plastic bottles (3), seawort, marram
grass, a length of rusted metal chain, thousands of
stones, 2 plastic bags, some shells, a rock, an orange
rope, moss, gorse, wet grass (muddy), rock samphire,
blue plastic piping, a broken pint glass (partly buried),
sudden gathering of terns, a lot of seaweed – mainly
knotted wrack and kelp, gritty sand, a gang of Canada
geese, unexpected, round a bend'

and she took photographs for him –

the wader she couldn't identify

the perfect reflection of a sheep

the evening light on the loch after rain

the view from the opposite shore

and she saw how they didn't interest him,
how they all looked the same.

A restless night, a storm, the threat of flood

A restless night, a storm, the threat of flood.
At 8am the ghostly wail of the siren and by midday
streets are flowing, steep roads surge.
Everything is river and the river is more than itself,
carrying vehicles on its back, a fallen tree, trying to
drag its feet to calm the rage but it's too headstrong,
churning silt and gravel, spewing up a pushchair,
plastic shoe, dead jackdaw, bin. Everything is brown
and broken. Everything is wet.

She's out with the rest of the town in wellies,
rubber gloves, remembering the last flood,
how he'd cursed his lack of strength to bail and lift,
how he'd driven instead, delivered food to homes
that were drowned and she knows she should be glad
he isn't seeing this.

Next day she walks the woods but her old path
is gone. Perhaps that's why she turns for home,
makes a list of everything she's shifted since he died,
imagines him coming back to the tidy house:
new doorbell, missing folders, mended light.
Would she run from room to room like an excited child,
show him what she's rearranged? Or apologise?

Getting the Last Word

MARTINA EVANS

Thomas McCarthy, *Poetry, Memory and the Party: Journals 1974–2014* (The Gallery Press) €20.00

'I am a deeply conservative person. I have been conservative since I was about seven-years-old,' Thomas McCarthy writes in May 2011 after a day spent at the Anglo-Irish writer Molly Keane's house in Ardmore, with Virginia her daughter and Lani, their literary advisor:

Maybe I'm too attached to these Anglo-Irish people and their houses: it's certainly true that I'm too attached for my own political and literary good. Everything in Irish life now eschews aristocracy and anything that smacks of grace or grandeur. My attachment to Molly Keane or the Brigadier's memory is among the most real emotional strings of my adult life. I have no hope of seeing this attachment reciprocated but that's not what it's about. It's something else, some very deep recognition of universal values that I also associate with a life of writing. For me writers, and especially poets, are born aristocrats – their instincts are value-laden, elitist in a technical sense, and associated with established comfort in that writing requires huge tranches of uninterrupted time the way that the making of a great garden or a great family requires centuries rather than moments of sensation.

There is something in the way that Thomas McCarthy pins his unfashionable colours to the mast that is engaging. Is McCarthy a 'true blue' conservative? That is debatable. Is love of beauty confined to conservatives? Is this conservatism political or cultural or can there even be a dividing line? It is true that writing does require 'huge tranches of uninterrupted time' but how many people are lucky enough to acquire this kind of time? Indeed, Thomas McCarthy's fascinating journals are testament to a life that was anything but uninterrupted.

Like a novel, the diaries begin in *medias res*; McCarthy is twenty, he has published poems in the *Irish Times* and is working as gardener for 'The Brigadier', Denis Fitzgerald, grandson of the Duke of Leinster. He has also won the support of one of Ireland's finest novelists, Molly Keane. Three pages into the diary, he writes that Keane has been 'urging' the Brigadier 'to find a job for me in London. She has taken a shine to me since I helped her with cuttings from the Kalmia latifolia, the calico bush, at Glenshelane.' She is the first of a line of great women in McCarthy's life to whom he never fails to pay tribute. The 'most real emotional strings' are already firmly and irrevocably tied. And I am reminded of my mother who grew up in County Limerick in an area intensely populated with Anglo-Irish aristocracy. She said, 'Anyone who ever worked for the gentry became like them.' Who could resist the support which McCarthy received from 'The Brigadier'? Who could resist this deep level of trust? The following entry was written when McCarthy was just twenty years old:

> *August 2nd 1974.* I was sitting in the sunshine on the patio at Glenshelane today reading the Brigadier's back copies of *Lloyds*...As I recited the names out loud the Brigadier filled me in on the background to each Lloyds member. This kind of education is certainly not available in the UCC English Department, or any English Department... The other day I said to him, 'How are you going to keep track of all these things when you retire and you no longer have the services of your secretary at Panmure Gordon?' He went into the house soon after that and came back with files... He went through letters and accounts for forty or so minutes. Then he looked at me and said: 'No, everything in order, everything in order. Shipshape.' He went off again and came back with a glass of sherry for both of us. (We'd successfully moved the Catalpa tree with its root-bowl intact, so he was pleased with himself.)

Very small clues are given as to what McCarthy's home-life is like. When the Brigadier comes home for St Patricks Day 1975, 'How wonderfully ordered his life... punctuated by holidays, festivals and commemorations. How I envy him his ordered life, constantly reaffirmed by public and regimental commemorations. As for my life, it is one continuous working-class daze... One of the absolutely distinguishing things about our family, the thing that marked us as underprivileged, was the complete lack of response to public events. The poor don't participate in a public realm. A family in poverty is always inward-looking, self-obsessed...' The paucity of details about McCarthy's homelife is frustrating at first especially when life with the Brigadier is so richly delineated with snippets of conversations from political and practical discussions right down to the minute descriptions of flowers, gardens, wine and food. In fact, McCarthy's brother Kevin asks later why McCarthy hasn't written more about his own family. 'But my unwillingness to exclude the world of the Brigadier, for instance, really annoys some people, even Cathy, even my brother Kevin, who wish well for my work.'

Yet, as the diaries progress, these silences ultimately prove to be very potent, especially on the rare occasions when McCarthy's feelings well up and he *must* speak, 'Dear God, the poor do flower early and are soon swept away. Not surprising that she should die inside two years of my father's death. Mutual suffering made them into one being. The rage I feel is unbelievable. I will never be able to write anything that is the equal of this intense rage. I think of all the forces in Irish life that oppressed and ruined her every waking hour. But for the poor there is no evil force as oppressive as the relentless force of poverty itself... My mother in her coffin looked very, very old – compressed years of excessive cruelty and hard-

ship. The world of poverty had cut so deep into her life, so furrowed and wrinkled her brow.' McCarthy is just twenty-five.

Further on, there is an unforgettable passage when he encounters a New Age Travellers' truck broken down on the avenue to Glenshelane House on a cold October evening in 1995. He describes the 'roar of the Glenshelane River in full spate... I think the roar of the river frightened the mother more than anything: there is such murderous power in a swift flow of flood water. Although it was only 6 p.m. it was dark. The scene was like a picture taken from my own life when I was seventeen or eighteen. That dripping, cold darkness of a West Waterford adolescence. And the appalling desolation I felt at having been born poor.'

The diaries cover forty years of Irish literary life. History and politics are vital players here too as they are in McCarthy's poems. But the overriding theme is the place of the poet within the world, the dangers of the world and how the poet negotiates those dangers. There is an astonishing force of feeling here and the reader cannot fail to be struck by it. It is an act of faith, an act of bravery to show one's own private thoughts to the world exactly as they are in all their inconsistencies, their strengths *and* weaknesses. More than any other literary genre, one has to be prepared to be misunderstood – Anthony Trollope paid dearly when he revealed his workmanlike approach to his own writing, the powers-that-be relegated him to the second division of novelists. But McCarthy has never been afraid to expose himself, his choice of Fianna Fail as a poetic subject remains to be fully appreciated. Trollope, of course, like McCarthy, had a family to support. Trollope worked for the post office, McCarthy worked at Cork City library, 'the shallow grave of Cork City Council...' There is a sense that McCarthy – like the radical diarist Claude Fredericks – sees the diary as a 'total' work of literature. McCarthy was studying other writers intensely from an early age, their journals are mentioned regularly from the very beginning of his own journal – Koestler, Gide, Seferis, Arnold Bennet, Stendhal and many more. He has studied the genre, feels at home in it and wonders why it disturbs others:

> What is it about us in Ireland that we fear these memoirs and diaries? We react to published memoirs as if they were all written as deliberate betrayals. You meet no person more outraged in Ireland than someone who's been remembered in a published book or diary. Why are we like this? Is it some deep peasant mistrust of openness, a horror of someone educated divulging tribal secrets?

In 1988, he writes of 'a brilliant review of a Catherine Cookson book' in the *Observer* – it is written by Anita Brookner 'with this interesting insight – Autobiography is traditionally a genre peculiar to the upwardly mobile, the socially insecure, those who have no context to explain them. Its purpose is to expunge pain, but more than this, to create a life myth, an alternative support system.' McCarthy refuses to create 'a myth' even though he applauds the publication of Frank McCourt's *Angela's Ashes*, which embraced the 'myth' – poles apart from

McCarthy in its approach to a childhood of poverty:

> Frank McCourt has won the Pulitzer Prize for his... harrowing account of his poor Limerick childhood and an angry indictment of the disgusting Catholic 'respectable' classes of that city... His success fills me with glee... he reminds me of Patrick Galvin, of Galvin's *Song for a Poor Boy*. Like me McCourt has a keenly polished chip on his shoulder because of a bitterly difficult childhood. But he doesn't have Patrick Galvin's deep sense of socialism, internationalism and class solidarity. Galvin makes me feel ashamed of my own lack of belief in a broad Left, in revolution, in Cuba, in an international Popular Front. McCourt is just a lone trader in literature like me, a cornershop owner, a small proprietor of his own home-grown miseries: a man alone. Paddy Galvin will never feel alone: he is loved instinctively, universally, by all the socialist young of Ireland.

What's interesting about McCarthy's journals is that they can hold two opposing views in a way which a tidied-up, carefully-edited autobiography never could. This is what makes them so utterly human. The 'Catholic "respectable" classes' of Limerick are not always 'disgusting'. McCarthy is absolutely charmed by Limerick middle-class women here:

> I met Joan and Joe McBreen, old Galway friends, and Jo Slade, the Limerick poet, an exquisitely beautiful and elegant Limerick woman. Middle-class Limerick women are truly extraordinary; they are like women of the Veneto, fine featured, well-bred, and moving through this world with a sublime social confidence.

I am reminded of an early entry in 1974 when Tom brings two friends – Bill Wall and Liz, a first cousin of Tom's friend, the poet Seán Dunne – to meet the Brigadier, 'The Brigadier very impressed by Bill and Liz. "Are they not the most superior young people, really most charming?" he remarked as they sped way down the avenue. The Brigadier loves good social breeding...'

Somehow I feel there is a hint of mischief in McCarthy's admiration of 'superior' people. I get the sense McCarthy likes to get a rise out of his readers as surely as some part of him seems to enjoy recounting this incident at Cork City Library on St Patricks Day, 1999:

> Today a photo in the *International Herald Tribune* of Prince Edward wearing a bunch of shamrock as he celebrates St Patrick's Day with the Irish Guards in Germany. I showed the photograph to a colleague at work thinking she'd be pleased. 'The bastard!' she exclaimed. 'Imagine that bastard appropriating our nation's symbol!'... I do walk on very thin ice with all my contradictory friendships and loyalties.

I found I had the same initial reaction as McCarthy's colleague when I read this but then I couldn't help laughing at myself too. These journals shake the reader, McCarthy forcing us to look again at our own biases even if we don't agree with his.

The poet Seán Dunne was one of his earliest friends at U.C.C. but it was a friendship that proved to be treacherous. In 1997 McCarthy writes, 'Lar Cassidy of the Arts Council has died... He was always a little bit suspicious of me, because of the Fianna Fáil material... Probably seriously misinformed about me by Seán Dunne as well, in that understated but treacherous way Seán had of convincing people that I'd just had dinner with some Fianna Fáil Himmler or Goebbels.'

Not surprisingly, in a diary which is primarily concerned with the position of the poet in the world, Heaney's name crops up more than any other poet, over two hundred times. McCarthy was an observer, admirer and supporter of Heaney from his early days at U.C.C. when he studied under John Montague. Montague, like the Brigadier, was another supportive father figure in McCarthy's life and McCarthy in his turn supported and took care of Montague and the Brigadier right up until the end of both their lives. In 1975, after the publication of Heaney's *North,* McCarthy comments, 'In terms of public profile [Heaney... is now light years ahead of the Irish pack, so far ahead that he doesn't even hear them snapping at his ankles.'

The nature of fame preoccupies McCarthy from the earliest pages of the journal, no doubt because it preoccupied Montague too. McCarthy writes how Montague feared Heaney's success and predicted as early as 1980 that Heaney would win the Nobel Prize. Montague's 'depression is certainly connected with this drink problem, a fear of ageing, a fear of the power of Seamus Heaney ('Heaney's ascendancy is still blamed for everything: Kinsella's illness, Murphy's darkness, Mahon's drinking) and the difficulties of writing *The Dead Kingdom*, particularly 'The Black Pig' sequence. I feel incapable of helping him when he gets into this King Lear mood. Nobody can help while he's raging against all these imaginary storms of the literary world.' There are times when McCarthy's observations on Heaney set against the envy of other Irish poets are actually frightening, 'In literature, as in the theatre, envy is first cousin of imagination. The crowd that waits for Heaney to stumble grows and grows.' The joy and excitement of Heaney's Nobel prize, so astutely predicted by Montague, is described in great detail but this shocking entry from 1995 stays in the mind – Heaney has just finished a reading at U.C.C.:

> When I recited a few lines of 'Exposure' behind his back he swung round and clasped my hand. His hair wispy and snow-white, his voice nearly gone from all the talking since he was awarded the Nobel Prize. It probably won't be possible to have a real conversation with him for two years or more – until the white heat of international fame has cooled. Because of fame he is not really in full possession of himself: the distracted and distrusting world owns him. The look of exhaustion in his eyes, a collapse of the face, was quite frightening to see. But this is fame: what every desolate poet dreams of having. The problem is this: fame is not an optional state, it will not go away when one's need for it is satiated. His face and eyes had the look of a great library that had been ransacked already by vicious thieves and vandals.

McCarthy is as loyal to Heaney as he is to the West Waterford aristocracy. Loyalty and service are the main qualities which characterise these journals and not just for the Brigadier or Montague but for literature, for family and for the Cork City of Culture 2005, for which he gave five years of his life.

There is one other overwhelming loyalty – and that is McCarthy's lifelong support and promotion of women. His wife Cathy is central to the diaries and in one of the most touching passages in the diaries he describes the death of her beloved mother Kitty Coakley. Here the poet and novelist join effortlessly, as with almost casual economy, he reveals the deepest emotion.

Then Kitty rallied at around 9 o'clock, after her sister, Mary Corbett, a nun in Liverpool, came home. Kitty said, 'Hello Tom' to me when I walked into the room. She was that alert, at such a late stage of dying. She commented to one member of the family: 'I suppose I should be sad but I suppose it'll hit me tomorrow.' The supreme irony and aptness of the comment are typical of Kitty's best 'bon mots'. She was an absolute master of the understatement.

He is always conscious of Irish women's place in the world, too. This is unusual for an Irish male poet of his generation. From his early years at Iowa in 1980 where he met Jane Cooper, he is thinking about the women. When he discovers Cooper's ground-breaking, feminist essay, 'Nothing Has Been Used in the Manufacture of This Poetry That Could Have Been Used in the Manufacture of Bread,' he immediately photocopies it and sends it back to Ireland, '...it contains urgent insights about women as poets, really crucial, empowering insights that could stiffen the resolve of women poets in Cork. The important thing is to get this text to them before their confidence is destroyed by the provincial masculinities, the pathetic masculinities, of influential poets operating locally.' His opinions haven't changed by 2005 when he is on the board of the Cork2005 programme:

So I have kept my promise to myself at the beginning of the year. With €131,000 in the bag for them we've made an historical response to the women who run the Tig Filí and Cork Women's Poetry Circle. This is the first time that these women, my heroes since the early 1980s, will have proper budgets to work with. They have never been taken seriously, yet the work Máire Bradshaw has done in literature and society in Cork is the most important literary work of the last half century. Why haven't my male companions ever admitted this achievement? It's as if they'd longed for its failure. I think there are many men, and many literary men, who long to see women fail.

Apart from his writer and artist wife, Cathy, whose achievements and character are celebrated right through the journals, there is one woman writer who burns from these pages and that is Molly Keane, who took such a great interest in him when he was a young gardener at Glenshelane. McCarthy's description of the unexpected success of her novel *Good Behaviour* in 1981 just when it seemed like she might be 'a spent force' is one of the most acute in the journals:

September 12th Last night BBC Radio 4 announced that Molly Keane's book has been shortlisted for the Booker Prize. The turnaround in her career has convinced me that anything of real value, like *Good Behaviour*, will be justly treated in the end. A writer or poet identifies all the usual enemies – bad publishers, poor distributors, demanding friends, personal exhaustion – in an effort to explain the neglect of work, only to discover that the main enemy is within oneself, a tendency merely to vegetate. Success changes one's image of a writer. I always thought of Molly Keane as an old lady, terribly bothered and slightly tipsy, asking me if her chihuahua, 'Hero', could sleep with her in her bedroom at Glenshelane. I always thought of her battered old Morris Minor, later an old Renault 4, setting off in the rain to go back to the loneliness of Ardmore. Then, when I learned that first Collins in London and then Mercier Press in Cork had turned down early drafts of her new novel, I felt that she was finished, a spent force. But, now, how her image has brightened! Every day she's in the newspapers, blazing with a new authority. Her life has been renewed in old age but she has also been renewed in my mind's eye, even in memory. And, among the resident Ascendancy families in the Blackwater Valley, she has been reborn: even they are quickly scrambling to revise their memories of her.

McCarthy recognises all that is brilliant in Molly Keane's work: he writes about her novel, *The Rising Tide*, 'There is nothing as powerful as the integrity of a completely imagined world.' He has been a lifelong supporter of her work, yet another service he's performed – making sure that Keane's legacy is safe, 'What a magical presence she was, our own Edith Wharton; what joy knowing her brought into my life.'

And yet, those early years are still shrouded. Are more journals yet to come to light? Readers of this volume will surely want more, along with answers to so many questions– Is Cathy still writing short stories? How did Seán Dunne turn so many of McCarthy's friends against him? Like a real life, there are so many missing pieces and it is true that if one sat down from one end of the day to the other, one could not set down every moment in a life – and that's what makes it all so tantalising. If only we could ask Molly about young Tom – that would be a very special literary treat. All we know is that Molly gets the last word with a bit of help from another favourite writer:

As Isaac Bashevis Singer once wrote, a life of writing is the same as a life dedicated to the study of the Talmud – it is its own reward. A life in writing may be endlessly hand-to-mouth, but it is full of life. As Molly Keane used to say – holding a champagne Martini or a Bloody Mary aloft in front of the blazing drawing-room fire at Glenshelane House – to write is hell, but not to write is even worse.

The Silent Songs of the Walls

ULRIKE ALMUT SANDIG

Translated from the German by Karen Leeder

of a chapel next to Tiefenau Castle, which is completely invisible,
as it was blown up in 1948, heard on a day in the twenty-first century with few visitors.

I

I have the same number of words inside me
as all of you have words, the exact same number

but how many times can they be combined? you
keep finding words that no one sang before you.

your godhead made you after his own image
stark naked, blind – wild things that you are.

I am naked and blind too. my heart is of stone.
you flit in and out, grow larger, have

young and soon grow smaller again, smaller
until you can no longer be seen in your forests

made of gold-leaf and stone. in sinus curves
of a perfectly uniform tone you come and go

come and go through the centuries.
every one of your words I have stored in my

walls. little gods of mine! have you made me
after your own image? in the symmetry of right

and left and a perfect third thing
that is simply invisible – or empty?

II

I have so many words inside me
as many as murder ballads. in my emptiness

how the Silbermann organ resounds, when a local girl
fetches the giant key from the farm next door

and plays through the night, just for the rose garden
full of roses and lilac, roses, martens and goose feathers

I have so many pipes in me, so many clowns, I could
sound like a karaoke chapel in a club in Kyoto!

listen to the silent registers behind the wooden curtain
listen with hands over your ears. they are playing the litanies

of right and wrong. here an example of wrong:
do you see the castle before my entrance portal?

you don't? it stands neither to left nor right
like the plundered goods you find in homes here abouts

for who would want to let the good dressers
explode? I am the castle chapel without a castle.

you martens – with eyes closed you stare
at the beautiful staircases made of air

III

I have so many words inside me
as many as three centuries of Our Father on a loop.

                    once a year the local women come to make
             me beautiful. don't wash the mouths of your little ones

out with soap. use it to wash your
own hands. my walls record your prayers

             curses and rose laugher down through the centuries.
                  once (that was today) I spoke to you

you people who need your houses that you can lock
to call on your godhead, about whom you say

                  he is everywhere. and indeed he is everywhere.
                  once the stone marten came up to my attic

it sounded like the riders of the apocalypse in training
for the end of days. and when the summer had passed

                  the universe simply looked right through me
            the roof was so leaky. and when the winter had passed

I had three small stone marten young
they were naked and blind, for your godhead

had made them in his own image

Three Poems

KUDZAI ZINYEMBA

Mount St Helens

We all stand on the porch and take pictures as if we've never seen fire before.
Men pour out of the warehouse exits, coughing and spattered with soot.
The flames themselves never cross the threshold.
I wouldn't notice it was burning except for the smoke –
a column the width of the building escaping through the atomized roof.
It coils as it rises, swirling thick and black and red.
Above us, the sun disappears.

Firemen come. They make calls. They field cameras.
The building is still burning ten hours later.
It's dry and January, grass crunching underfoot.
Crowds disperse in search of central heating.
Workmen turn their hands towards the blaze.
At dusk, the fire engines call it quits.
I check the mail before retreating. My letterbox is powdered gray.
The smoke column grows bigger each hour.

Green Thumb

In spring, rabbits nest in the east corner of the yard, sheltered by evergreen bushes.
They're hiding from coyotes – we now have a 'coyote problem'.
The arrival of coyotes had solved the town's 'deer problem',
which had previously solved the problem of a severe *lack* of deer
leaving the underbrush to grow haywire and the squirrels to lose track of their nuts.
It stings like eighth grade biology, like nitrogen fixation and deciduous food chains.
I never got the hang of photosynthesis. My tomatoes never grew.

Westward, a mulberry tree has been barren since birth.
The weather won't cooperate and neither will my father,
unwilling to mulch the soil by the roots.
Instead he prunes the grape vines. He fiddles with his eggplants.
He waters the hanging pots and picks off leaves of mint.
Beyond the tilled plots, the ground is awash with thistle, inaccessible when barefoot.
Our neighbors wear flip-flops when they sneak through the back,
beyond which lies the local pond, rife with frogs and bluegill.
Young boys carry buckets and rods. They are sunburnt by May.
I tell my father not to mend the broken fence.

Back to the tomatoes – it was my fault in the end.
Wasps settled in-between the siding and gardening meant getting stung.
The town is overrun with wasps. The air above the playground always buzzes.
Unlike coyotes, the dominance of insects never wanes.
Beneath the mulberry tree, ants pick apart a newborn chick, fallen from its nest.
Its mother has been missing for days. Her babies chirp all hours of the night.
At least its body will decay into ammonium, will fertilize the mangled roots.
Next year, there may even be whispers of fruit.

Ghost Ranch

My friend is in New Mexico, studying geology.
Every day at noon I get a phone call about nothing.
I must've lost five pounds by now. I'm wearing out my shoes.
She has a gift for burying the lede.
Four months ago, back East, she taught me how to mark striation.
She gifted me some sandstone, just for fun.
There must be sandstone in the desert
(I kind of thought that's all there is)
but two weeks in I'm left to guess it's not worth mentioning.
I glean little of the landscape – all she tells me is specifics.
I know she helps feed chickens, does her laundry, catches bugs.
She sends out of focus photographs of landforms in the distance
and follows up with jokes about the vultures in the air.
In undergrad we'd lunch together and she'd ramble about crystals.
She'd said geology was mostly about rocks.
It might be different when it's field work. I wouldn't know regardless.
Discussing her own research seems a chore.
My partner's such a buzzkill. He's obsessed with getting data.
She leaves me feeling I've misunderstood her job.
More importantly, she tells me, *I think the sunset here is gorgeous.*
I hum to show attention.

A Wary Friendship: Alfred Kazin and Robert Lowell

TONY ROBERTS

Over the course of thirty years Kazin, (1915–98) and Lowell (1917–77) learned to appreciate each other's considerable talent, despite their personal and political differences. After early setbacks, Kazin proved frequently effusive in his praise of Lowell – in public and in private – as we see from his books and his *Journals* (2011). After the poet's death he would concede certain weaknesses in the work and particularly in the man. For Lowell, on the other hand, Kazin provided an interesting, discriminating reader and a friendly audience.

Kazin, the radical critic, and Lowell, the conservative poet ('I have never been a Liberal tho I have a liberal vein') shared an absorption in American history, which they romanticized in their different ways. The son of impoverished Jewish immigrants, Kazin saw America as rich with promise, though a promise perilously close at times to being broken. His greats were the isolated literary radicals of the nineteenth century – Emerson, Thoreau, Whitman and Melville – outsiders like himself. 'The past, the past was great: anything American, old, glazed, touched with dusk at the end of the nineteenth century, still smoldering with the fires lit by the industrial revolution, immediately set my mind dancing' (*A Walker in the City*). Lowell, a patrician New Englander, was also a patriot, but one who in his early work seemed to relish castigating America as a fallen world, rich in sin and violence, and in need of redemption:

> Our fathers wrung their bread from stocks and
>   stones
> And fenced their gardens with the Redman's bones;
> Embarking from the Nether Land of Holland,
> Pilgrims unhoused by Geneva's night,
> They planted here the Serpent's seeds of light
> ('Children of Light')

A formidable networker, supportive of his many correspondents, Lowell kept a close eye on the literary scene, which included critic friends like Randall Jarrell, Allen Tate, William Empson, Al Alvarez, Edmund Wilson and his literary heir, Kazin. He prided himself on not losing any friendships (the delusional Delmore Schwartz's aside). As he remarked in a letter to Elizabeth Bishop in 1959, 'I think, perhaps I have more warm intellectual friends than anyone... But it's like walking on eggs. All of them have to be humored, flattered, drawn out, allowed to say very petulant things to you'. On occasion Lowell could even summon his part-Jewishness as a credential ('I'm one-eighth Jewish myself, which I do feel is a saving grace'). Despite his positive pronouncements on Jewish cultural influence, one comment obviously rankled with Kazin, since he referred to it twice in published work: 'Only Lowell was capable of saying of Jewish writers who were just as saturated in American life and literature as himself: "They have finally unloaded their European baggage."'

It is perhaps unfair to contrast Lowell's heartfelt letters to Bishop with Kazin's *Journals* ('The fact is that the journals scare even me when I look them over – so much longing, so much resentment' – 27 July 1989). In fact, they are a tribute to his frankness and probably more in line with the *mea culpa* tone of Lowell's post-breakdown letters and certain poetic moods. Yet even a look in the index reveals repeated entries for insecurities, intellectual uncertainty, psychoanalysis, self-criticism and social discomfort. Kazin, brilliant, doubtless charming, was ever troubled and always wary. His upbringing did not offer him the social insouciance Lowell could take for granted.

Politically, the two had little in common. In a letter of 15 January 1949 to George Santayana, Lowell had written 'I had a long argument the other evening with a fellow named Alfred Kazin. I said I couldn't imagine "Socialism" (he favors the liberal international kind...) has anything one could "believe in." It's a technique, necessary in various degrees, but depending on its context and qualifications for its value.' Lowell felt himself closer in 'sensibility' to T.S. Eliot. Kazin may have been nonplussed. He would later write, concerning the poet's friendship with Hannah Arendt, 'I was never to understand what Lowell's politics were.'

They would meet cordially from time to time, but on two early occasions their views clashed dramatically. In 1948 Ezra Pound received the Bollingen Library of Congress Award for the *Pisan Cantos*. Pound at the time remained confined in a mental hospital for his anti-Semitic, Fascist propaganda from wartime Italy. The award committee, including Eliot, Auden, Tate and Lowell, had voted for him in the belief that his work rather than his behaviour had been worthy of the award. Their decision proved highly contentious. As one of those canvassed for his views by *Commentary* magazine, Kazin pointed out that most Jewish intellectuals were fascinated by the very modernists who were anti-Semitic: he mentioned Dostoevsky, James, Henry Adams, Gide, Santayana, Cummings, Céline, Eliot and Pound. He believed that the isolated modern writer hated the Jews for that same isolation (a condition that R.P. Blackmur also touched on in an essay on Joyce's *Ulysses* in which he described the Jew as Everyman the outsider: 'in each of us, in the exiled part, sits a Jew').

Writing eleven years later Kazin, who by now had followed his precociously brilliant debut, *On Native Ground* (1942), with the first of his admired autobiographical trilogy, *A Walker in the City* (1951), expressed his criticism of Pound more forcefully. While recognizing that the young might be drawn to the poet as 'aged hipster and clown', he offered the following: 'Any man of good will *must* be divided about Pound. For myself, surrounded as I am by inexpungible memories of the millions of dead, I cannot think of the purely literary case made out for Pound without horror.' In his 1961 interview with Frederick Seidel, for *The Paris Review*, Lowell posed the opposite view. The committee had believed in the book, he argued, and 'the consequences of not giving the best book of the year a prize for extraneous reasons, even terrible ones in a sense – I think that's the death of art'.

The following year Kazin and Lowell clashed publicly, this time over the allegiances of the director of Yaddo, the writers' colony in Saratoga Springs, New York. Lowell had enjoyed his first visit to the retreat in the summer of 1947. There again in October 1948, after his stint as poetry consultant to the Library of Congress, he had written cheerfully of it. He lived in rooms of the farmhouse, Yaddo itself being 'an enormous mansion'. Here he met his future wife, Elizabeth Hardwick, and befriended Flannery O' Connor. He ate and played ping pong with the other guests. However, all was to change shortly as Lowell entered a manic phase, his condition read as exhilaration by those who did not know him well.

According to Lowell's biographer, Ian Hamilton, 'If, in his already "wound up" state, and with the Pound business in the air, Lowell needed an immediate target for his political hostilities, then Yaddo could hardly have been more obliging.' Agnes Smedley, a journalist with sympathy for the communist forces in China's civil war (a war nearing its end) had been a long-term guest at Yaddo and a friend of its administrator, Elizabeth Ames. In February 1949 *The New York Times* printed a false allegation that Smedley was a spy and Soviet agent. The army soon distanced itself from their report, which had prompted the accusation. The newspaper recanted; Smedley publicly thanked the army for clearing her name. Nevertheless FBI agents travelled to Yaddo to interview Elizabeth Hardwick and another guest.

Seizing this as an initiative, Lowell demanded the Yaddo board of directors dismiss Ames as 'a diseased organ, chronically poisoning the whole system'. In what he saw as his anti-Communist crusade, he threatened the public involvement of a number of highly influential literary friends. The following month Ames was officially exonerated, her reputation defended by a group including Kazin (for whom she had been 'a devoted friend to many writers over the years'). Lowell was censured. Shortly after this (and other highly wrought episodes) he had been confined in Baldpate, a private hospital near Georgetown, Massachusetts.

It seems ironic that during the war Kazin should have confided in his journal, 'I learned something at Yaddo – I learned a new sympathy for writers. I felt a new solidarity with all the lonely men in the lonely rooms' (June 1942). The world had changed since then; the War had turned 'Cold'. If Lowell had been 'wound up' for the Yaddo episode, Kazin himself – according to his autobiography *New York Jew* (1978) – hardly felt like tolerating what seemed to him a prevalent hysteria: 'The demand for orthodoxy suffocated me. Almost everywhere you looked now, the lies of Stalinists and the blood lust of super-Americans yelled down everything else.' Among the worst had to be the writers: 'The artist under political stress was an unforgettable picture of limitless self-regard'.

Lowell had been both dangerous and an irritant to Kazin: Though 'no longer a Catholic... he sounded like Evelyn Waugh rampaging against the wartime alliance with Russia. He objected more to Russia than to the war. It was a gloomy time for me; listening to Lowell at his most blissfully high orating against Communist influences at Yaddo and boasting of the veneration in which he was held by those other illiberal great men Ezra Pound and George Santayana, made me feel worse.' He would describe it in a review of Hamilton's biography for *The Times Literary Supplement* (6 May 1983) as his 'most jarring experience' with Lowell.

On a personal level, however, the matter would be dropped. In March 1953 the two met again at Oberlin College, Ohio, where Lowell deputized for Allen Tate, and where they both 'had made an effort to be civil', as Lowell mentioned in a letter to Tate. Their last reference to the Yaddo episode came on 3 October 1966, when Kazin records in his *Journals* in a conciliatory tone the dangers of Lowell's excitement: 'Lunch with Cal Lowell at Fleur de Lis. Cal very subdued, at the bottom of his cycle – terribly affectionate with me, full of intellectual fondness. He was talking about the old Yaddo business, and for a moment tried to indicate how strange his fanaticism of then seems to him now. I found myself saying how far the river of history has carried us, how much it has changed'. Kazin then mused on the universal tendency to demand coherence ('The cruelty of change on a mind seeking *constants*').

The two men corresponded irregularly over the years. In the fascinating Bishop/Lowell correspondence (collected in *Words in Air*) we read Elizabeth Bishop's tart reference to Kazin (1 April 1958) after his recent piece in *The New York Times Book Review*, in which he had praised James Agee's *A Death in the Family* a little excessively for her taste: 'AK is getting just too sort of injured-sophistication for words – he sounds as if he were the only man in the USA who *appreciates* things.' While Bishop could be critical of Kazin, they had in fact been friends of sorts since her difficulties (with alcohol) at Yaddo in late 1950.

Kazin's *Contemporaries: Essays on Modern Life and Literature* (1963) drew their only sustained response, since the collection featured one essay of particular interest ('In Praise of Robert Lowell'). *Contemporaries* reproduced Kazin's review written at the time of the appearance of *Life Studies* in 1959. The essay began with an observation on the early poetry: 'Robert Lowell's poetic style has been marked by a peculiar force, one that might well have been called violence but for its learning, bookishness, and nostalgia for traditional order.' Kazin mentioned the poet's 'precision of passion', the 'formal beauty' of his style, and wrote of the literariness of the poems 'more intense about life than intimate with it'.

With *Life Studies*, he saw the 'native elegance' retained even when the style has been 'stripped'. Henry Adams served as a comparison. Both 'have the gift of experiencing and expressing their own situations to the depths'. Pound and Pound's master, Browning, are also invoked as influences in their 'overliterary inflation' and 'dash and speed', in 'stylizing the communion with self that is the essence of dramatic monologue'. In sum, Kazin declared: 'In these poems twentieth-century poetry comes back to its great tradition as plain speech; comes back, in Pasternak's phrase, "to its sister, life".'

Inevitably flattered, Lowell wrote to Kazin in March 1962, his delight at being admired typically freighted by the judicious observation: 'You seem to be the only critic beside Edmund [Wilson], who reads new books. I mean in some deep way they are relived inside you and come out again heavy with their old actuality, but reformed by your character and digestive system.'

As if searching for clarity here, Lowell continued: 'what strikes me is that you keep your own strong feeling, and prejudices and yet lose yourself in the difficulties of each writer. You neither let them swallow you, nor lecture them. What you say about my old too literary side is surely true. Let's all get together in the spring.' The postscript reiterated the admiration: 'I can't read one of your pieces without feeling changed'. This could be called criticism *quid pro quo*, Lowell's reference to Wilson being intended to thrill Kazin, whose admiration for the master remained infinite.

It is somewhat deflating then – and a peril of searching private letters – to read that in mid-April Lowell described the book to Bishop as a 'great heap of essays, surprisingly tougher and less long-winded than he is'. Bishop in her turn proved severe about them in her loyal response: 'The Kazin book I find infuriating but good in spots – the best spot being his review of you – the one really generous review in the whole book, I think. There must be thousands of "*I*"s in that book... and it's badly written, as well.'

Lowell is more generously treated in Kazin's *Journals*. The first reference is a punchy one-liner from 26 November 1946: 'Robert Lowell: the triumph of talent over confusion'. This appeared in the context of an entry about how the atomic bomb had invaded the thinking of everyone in post-war America. This feeling would be captured years later in Lowell's 'Fall 1961', the immediate context now being the Bay of Pigs debacle, when nuclear extinction was again in everyone's thoughts:

All autumn, the chafe and jar
of nuclear war;
we have talked our extinction to death.
I swim like a minnow
behind my studio window.

By the 1960s the relationship between poet and critic had been established on a firmer foundation. There is an element of intellectual exhilaration, even of hero worship, in one entry Kazin made in his journal in November 1965:

Late Saturday evening visit with Cal Lowell, my mad poet, my only genius. Cal excited by greatness, by comparing greatness. He is always making up verbal lists – the best historians, the best critics, the best stylists... Cal flitted easily from name to name and from subject to subject, but his sense of greatness, his sense of the great work, of the great moment in the great work, made me feel, again, as if I were breathing the unfamiliar, pure air at the mountain

peak. He said, among other wonderful things, that Satan is Milton's hero because Satan has such a great *voice*, like Milton.

Kazin's last recorded sighting of the poet in the *Journals* is on 19 November 1967 where he enthusiastically reports the following:

Here it is Sunday morning, gray and leaden, and suddenly Cal Lowell is on the phone talking about St. Paul and St. Louis and Cato the younger, moving in and out of history with what a perspective! Marvelous unprovincialism of the gifted man. Cal's new poems, especially the one about Caracas... show what a little radical experience can do for a poet! Great to have him reading these poems on the phone just now. What a privilege.

Lowell's 'radicalization' had been in evidence the previous month when he had taken part in a protest against the Vietnam War, which is now remembered as 'the March on the Pentagon'. He, Norman Mailer, Dwight Macdonald and 50,000 others had courted confrontation with paratroopers on guard at the headquarters of the Department of Defence across the Potomac from Washington, D.C. According to Edmund Wilson, in *The Sixties*, 'Cal said that it had been one of the fine moments of his life'. It is certainly one of the most remembered, thanks to Mailer's chronicle of their involvement, in *Armies of the Night* (1968) with its admiring portrait of Lowell as patrician poet.

It was probably to be expected that, as the critic, Kazin would puzzle over, consider or at least reference the work of the poet rather than that Lowell, as poet, would write of him. Kazin hardly appears in the published Lowell letters after this time and Lowell left for England in 1970. There is a sighting when Elizabeth Hardwick wrote to him there in August 1970 regarding her social life: 'Ann and Alfred Kazin have spent the summer near Blue Hill, which seems odd, and are coming over this afternoon. Alfred has been unkind about M. McC. and so nothing communal can be planned' (In *Starting Out in the Thirties* [1965] Kazin had been scathing about Mary McCarthy). The last reference in Lowell's published correspondence is admiring. In a letter of April 1973, he mentions 'Alfred's nostalgic but beautiful picture of the New York that has disappeared', in a piece Kazin had written for *The New York Review of Books*.

Lowell's death in September 1977 released Kazin from the desire to be discreet, and his remarks after that date betray an ambivalence, especially about the man. He acknowledged Lowell's talent in *New York Jew* in describing him as 'the strongest poet of my generation' (though adding that he was 'given to mood swings that encouraged his gift for exaltation'). He also admitted that Lowell's instinct for language worked on him 'with the force of a jackhammer'. The use of 'strongest' and 'jackhammer' reveal Kazin's preference for the kind of muscular style characteristic of the poet through much of his career.

To him, Lowell's experience had been symptomatic of the national experience: 'Poetry in America could never be anything but "personal," for the only tradition it had was American energy rather than the classical art of harmony.' And then Lowell carried a lot of family baggage with him, tradition and pressures which fascinated Kazin: 'The Lowell attic – the world of things – heirlooms – all that stuff, all those ancestors and relatives, associations and quotations, almost too many people to write *to*.'

In his review of the Ian Hamilton biography (*TLS*, 6 May 1983), Kazin wrote his most negative assessments of Lowell as poet and man. Time had passed. His earlier enthusiasm had obviously cooled somewhat as fashions changed. He noted that 'Among the poets only "Cal" was so familiar to readers who never met him, who didn't need to in order to gossip about him.' He saw this as an 'over-valuation of Lowell's "confessional" tone'. He went further: 'A net of allusiveness, fame and anxious name-dropping surrounded his poetry'. Coming to the heart of this, Kazin reckoned that the famous poems 'are not so much moving as "impressive". The most important feature of Lowell's poetic line is its tricky grace, its need to surprise, its demonstrativeness... Lowell performed all the time, soon it did not matter if the poem was weak so long as the line was "strong".'

This focus on the line in Lowell is, I think, accurate. What comes next, however, is severe: 'By nature he was a powerful, aggressive and altogether bossy person beset by manic depression and frightened even when, with his ventriloquist's skill, he wrote in a lordly voice alternating with a timid one.'

In his penultimate book, *Writing Was Everything* (1995), Kazin is kinder. While his ambivalence is clear ('Other poets needed praise; Lowell expected adoration'), he reaffirmed his faith in the poetry: 'I always forgave Lowell for taking on superior airs,' he wrote. 'His talent in a generation of poet wimps was vivid and strong, even if the learned allusions with which he began his career were derived from the southerners he adored so much.' Kazin also admire 'Lowell's immensely sophisticated ease in knowing when to rein in, his upper-class training in controlled conversation.' The reference to 'upper-class training' brings us back, once again, to the essential distance in affinity between the two men.

From the Archive

from *PNR* 237, Volume 44 Number 1, 2017

Self Portrait

Allow me this moment
all to myself. Doctor,

there was no room to breathe
at the family gathering;

thin-skinned and out of kilter
I ducked behind

a thick stone pillar
then slipped outside

to Facebook and vape.
Doc, it was a no-brainer:

airbrush my own face
out of the picture [...]

SIMON ARMITAGE

more available at www.pnreview.co.uk

A History

DAN BURT

I. VISIT 1

Philoctetes

I was not her high school sweetheart
(though she was mine), merely a *sans culotte*
strayed from the wrong side of the city
dated for a spring, dropped, forgot.

By chance we met again fifty years later.
In that span I reared a seaside pile
on a granite cliff Down East
with cedar shingles and tall glass to watch
the North Atlantic gnaw its rock,
laid down claret, vintage port,
lined the walls with unquiet post-war art –
at the foot of the grand stair, sixteen feet tall,
Kiefer's poisoned Rhine flowed across the wall –
and in that company dwelt on my sawdust past.

I asked her there to applaud my works.
On the patio over wine and waves
echoes of her girlish lilt
her irises still crystal blue
tore the bandage from the wound
that never knit exposing
an old spectral tableau –
a teenage butcher in too short cuffs,
smelling of suet Brut could not cloak,
standing before a princess on a Saturday night
suing hat-in-hand for love –
and shame and rage that seeped from it.

My mid-Atlantic vowels shrank,
high-table diction resiled to Philly slang,
and through clenched teeth I pooh poohed
the trappings she had come to view.
She raised her hand to pat my shoulder
as a mother might to calm a child.
I brushed it aside before she touched me
and went on staring out to sea.

II. VISIT 2

Yvonne de Galais

Sea spray lashed the windows
beside the table laid for two,
where candlelight danced in crystal
before a woman I barely knew.
Her ravined face across the silver,
thin grey curls, pale mottled skin
above hips splayed by parturition
guyed the vestal who had glistened
in reveries all my adult years.

She mapped the stations of her life
from our last teen date 'til tonight:
Ivy college, Sixties radical,
bra-less Harvard PhD,
Model Cities high school principal,
then, like many a sad Aquarian
back to the land to teach
mature students Jane Austen,
raise a daughter on her own
and kayak amongst the loons
on the Maine pond behind her home.

There were no coordinates for me.

Sie Kommt

(...*Es ist die Königin der Nacht*...)
   Tamino, *The Magic Flute*, Act 1, sc. 2

She comes trailing shadows never cast
by any earthly forms whose charge and mass
thwart light. They flutter just beyond my grasp
like cherry blossoms a puff of wind unclasps.

She comes around the corner of the years
streaming faux memories from foreign piers
that never were, dreams I fear
of unshared passages, landfalls, and tears.
She comes and for a breath regret unveils
fantasy tableaux: our first-born's squall,
trimming the sheets teaching her to sail,
her hand on mine before my father's pall.

Phantoms finning in canyons of my night
no magic flute can pipe you to the light.

Deposition

Tumour

Surgeons probe the ruin
that six weeks before was a woman
for the springs of her Nile of pain:
razed ovaries through a keyhole –
they proved benign;
twice hoovered her guts
through a nasogastric hose –
but still they fouled;
slit her abdomen at last
and from the colon cut
the egg-sized ruby mass
that damns her bowels.

Post-Op

Around the clock scrubs come and go,
check vital signs, the glucose drip,
bring clear liquids she can sip,
and tell us nothing we want to know.

By the bed her daughter and I stand
spin bad news into bland
walk off at times to hide
quivering lip, moistening eye
and dread the 'path' report
will ferry hope to Hell.

Mid-morning, mid-afternoon
the scarecrow hanging on my arm
shuffles speechless round the ward.
I hum *Va pensiero* under my breath
conjure the orchestra, hear
Nabucco's Hebrew slaves implore
the God I'm certain is not there.

Delphi

Nine storeys up the January sun
fills the oncology waiting rooms
lights pear wood chairs
beige carpets, off-white walls,
and pencil-thin, pale alopetes
whose cadaverous flesh
mocks their studied calmness.
Patient, daughter, and I sit
fidget, prattle, go for a pee
and feign no fear
the news will be
not what we want to hear.

The haruspex enters quietly
half-tied surgical gown awry
scuffed brown wing-tipped shoes,
shambling, portly distant man
his blank face, guarded gaze
tell he's acted the raven in too many plays:

You have Stage IV colon cancer. We couldn't find the source.
The surgeon who removed the blockage thinks he got it all,
but can't be sure.
When you recover a little more, we'll do
an endoscopy, and PET scan;
I doubt they'll change our view.
Chemotherapy's standard for what you have,
a six-months course, if you can stand it.
Then we review.

What will the chemo do?

Give you a year, maybe two....

Her late-life only child turns aside to sob
I flinch though the verdict's no surprise
and my wasted high school heartthrob
poleaxed, mute, empty eyed,
a stranger now, decouples from us
and boards her little black train.

Totentanz

Death settles on the exam table
as the oncologist bids good day,
flutters anthracite feathers,
eyes us, nods
then swings his new partner away.

Gathered in its tightening wingspan
gyring down the shadow path
she pries at the talons
that clamp her fast,
with chemicals, diet, all she can muster
to loosen them for a measure
though nothing can sever
this pair from their round together.

I am a wallflower at the dance
watching my lady slowly die
and as sigh treads on sigh
replay a sixty-year-old teen romance.

Coda

She paused, looking at him for
a moment with a smile. 'My name?
I am Mademoiselle Yvonne de Galais...'
Then she was gone.
  Le Grand Meaulnes, Alain-Fournier

We trudged under the lash of measurement
each pulse a question
Will the next scan be clear?
pursued by odds we'd too soon hear
Your cancer is past treatment.

Against that hour I sifted memory
honed on clarity
slow dancing with death brings,
not the last ten winter years
when we grew close
met again by hap as pensioners,
but three months as your subject
while you slummed it,
a pubescent uptown rose
experimenting with a bit of rough.

I refined myself
after that brief encounter,
quarried Wordsworth, Eliot, Lowell, Yeats,
cast your deities as mine
pictured us kneeling at their shrine,
but the conjunctive moment past
worshipped alone.

I'll sing no sad songs for you
my dearest when you are dead.
For *kaddish* I'll surrender
the rage loving you engendered
and the still-born dreams that drove me
lee-rail buried down the years.

i.m. Jill Rubinson
17/8/1943 – 30/7/2018

Rinasce

Violetta: *In me rinasce* –Act III, *La Traviata*

For the last time she rose unaided from her bed.
The ghost-white cotton shift she wore
eleven years before
when we first watched the sun
fire the Gulf of Maine at dawn
swamped her now, hem dragging the floor.
Three days later she was dead.

She clutched my forearms as I turned to leave,
steadied, breathed *You are the centre*
of my world. I love you
then buckled at the knees.
Ten last words
a whisper wrung from trachea
vocal cords and lips, a blessing.
We shared no issue, no gold rings
no locket with her portrait in enamelling
lay in some dresser to pass on.
All she could bequeath a puff of air
a confession I had played the lead
in her final decade's mortality
a charm to wield against my Furies.
  You are the centre of my world....
Three days later she lay dead.

V. COLONUS

The Lynam Graveyard

1
In a Yankee family graveyard
on a bluff Down East
above a cobble beach,
lime-yellow lichen cling
to seven words cut mid-way down
a flaking, knee-high, granite headstone.

John Alby
Co. E
8th Me. Infantry

To the left a span away
a palm-sized five-point pewter star
atop a rusted iron rod,
two points intact three just scar
embossed *Post 105, G.A.R.*
salutes the Union service of
a Mainer dead in blue.

From middle age most mornings
I passed the spot
coffee mug in hand still hot
but never lingered
gave that blue-boy's bones a thought
or marked the *shushhh* that rose
from pebbles the tide bowed
back and forth across the hard below,
a scowling Rhadamanthine passer-by,
horizons cropped by butcher-boy years
and passage from trade to corner-suite
who looked on life like Macbeth –
cacophony and nothingness.

3

A dodderer now
I sometimes pause
by John Alby's grave,
wonder who he was
or might have been,
listen to the tidal hissing's rise and fall
two stories down in the cove ahead,
even catch when elements align
faint still sad music
in what had seemed
a mere distempered symphony,
my world rescored alchemically
by weekends with a lady
in her life's last decade
encountered again in my silver years
after she had enchanted me as a boy,
by the final bedside vigil
her skeletal hand limp in mine
as breath haltingly withdrew
and by grief
her absence each day renews.

NOTE

G.A.R. stands for Grand Army of the Republic, a fraternal society for Union Civil War Veterans founded
in 1866, a year after the end of the American Civil War. See Wikipedia for an image of a G.A.R. memorial
star. Union soldiers wore blue uniforms, and American southerners still refer to them as *blue boys*.

Reviews

The Mechanical Bard

Mike Sharples and Rafael Pérez y Pérez, *Story Machines: How Computers Have Become Creative Writers* (Routledge) £14.99
Reviewed by Nicolas Tredell

'Je ne suis qu'une machine à faire des livres.' Thus Chateaubriand, perhaps expressing a widespread feeling among writers, at least prolific ones, that they sometimes tend towards the condition of the mechanical and perhaps may even aspire to it as an escape, albeit illusory, from the fluctuations of personality and the accidents of existence. Sartre applies Chateaubriand's description to himself in his autobiography, *Les Mots* (1964), echoing the mechanical imagery in his 1938 novel, *La Nausée*, where Antoine Roquentin experiences a rare epiphany that momentarily sets unfenced existence in order: 'je sens mon corps comme une machine de précision au repos'. This calm supervenes when listening to a song rather than writing a story, but it could also fit the latter experience in those moments when the words flow and fall into place with a kind of vibrant exactitude that is aesthetically pleasing, existentially concordant and quite possibly, as Sartre suggested in *Les Mots*, a mighty self-deception, a misplaced and impossible quest for salvation through language.

Such a deception might look even greater if there were indeed machines that could make books. We are not quite there yet, as Mike Sharples and Rafael Pérez y Pérez acknowledge in their informed and intriguing study *Story Machines: How Computers Have Become Creative Writers*; but the possibility no longer sounds improbable or inhuman. F.R. Leavis once insisted, in a characteristic flight of cognitive hubris, that he knew a computer could not write a poem and saw the very idea that it was pos-

sible to do so as an index of the cultural depths to which technologico-Benthamite society had sunk; but this was in the days when computers were still hulking beings of heavy metal, housed in huge rooms with reinforced floors to bear their weight, performing mysterious night jobs that would issue during the day in copious data. They still belonged on the wrong side of that rigid binary distinction, deriving from Romantic aesthetics, between the organic and the mechanical, with the latter perceived as '*une machine infernale*' of clanking cog wheels, whirling belts, thrusting pistons, viscous lubricants and gouts of steam. Computers, it was believed, could never compete with, let alone surpass, human intelligence, and were dependent on human beings for their creation and continued existence. They would short-circuit and self-destruct in a burst of sparks and fumes if faced with a question like 'Why?' and could never beat a human chess master, let alone write a poem.

This easy assignment of computers to subaltern status, however, is no longer plausible. Computers are far quicker at many mental operations than human beings; they can be self-replicating and self-repairing; it hardly seems science-fictional now to envisage a scenario in which silicon-based beings survive when carbon-based beings have long vanished. Today's computers are not necessarily fazed by supposedly difficult questions, even if their answers may not seem, in human terms, quite adequate (like '42' as the answer to the question of life, the universe and everything returned by the megacomputer Deep Thought in Douglas Adams's *The Hitchhiker's Guide to the Galaxy*); and they can see off a human chess master, even if, as Sharples and Pérez y Pérez point out, 'they operate in very different ways from the human mind by grinding through millions of possible moves rather than by assessing patterns and strategies'.

Moreover, twenty-first-century digital technology, though it can produce surface manifestations of peerless vivacity, is scarcely visible or audible in its crucial underlying operations; it needs no dark satanic mills, and does not seem alien, other, impersonal. Without denying the reality of digital poverty, such technology now weaves itself into the very substance of most people's lives, felt in the blood and felt along the heart, facilitating and shaping the seemingly spontaneous overflow of powerful feelings; it can appear to have magical and oneiric qualities; and it generates stories. For example, even the briefest tweet can spark off a multivoiced narrative, a many-stranded thread that, rather than offering, like Ariadne's twine, a way back out of the labyrinth, leads ever more deeply into its increasingly intricate passages and cunning corridors. Of course, many of these threads are still human-authored, though bots, some capable of passing the Turing Test, may also play a prominent part. But in today's world it hardly requires a large imaginative leap to believe that a computer, 'a mechanical bard' as this book calls it at one point, could write a poem or a story, or indeed to credit Nick Bostrom's argument, in his much-discussed 2003 paper, that we are all characters in a computer-scripted simulation.

In *Story Machines*, Sharples and Pérez y Pérez point out that the desire to create machines that can write stories and poems is not new: John Peter's pamphlet *Artificial Versifying, or the Schoolboy's Recreation: A new way to make Latin verses* appeared in 1677, and it still seems possible, following its rather complex instructions, to generate passable Latin hexameters by means of it. In the mid-nineteenth century, inventor and poet John Clark designed the Eureka, 'a machine for making Latin verses' exhibited at the Egyptian Hall in Piccadilly in 1845, which could likewise generate Latin hexameters, though not very meaningful ones. Sharples and Pérez y Pérez make the interesting point that Clark used the kaleidoscope as his 'model for creative composition' because it combined 'random alignment and constrained patterns'.

In the early 1960s, Joseph Grimes programmed the first automated storyteller, and the tales he produced had the kind of features identified in Vladimir Propp's *Morphology of the Folktale* (1928; trans. 1958); but they were too minimalist and minuscule to count fully as stories. In the 1970s. Sheldon Klein and his fellow researchers drew directly on Propp to create stories that seemed like folk tales. Recently, the programme GPT-2 and, even more powerfully, GPT-3, were generative language networks that had the capacity to produce plausible stories (including dangerously persuasive 'fake news' stories). The authors of this book asked GPT-3 to generate an ultra-short story, first for adults and then for children, and it did so, although its stories, in their view, 'don't quite make sense' or show a full cognitive grasp of the workings of the world. One of the ultra-short stories they use to exemplify this, however, a dialogue between a husband who receives a phone call from an insurance company to say that they cannot accept his wife's life insurance because, apparently unbeknown to him, she is dead, is rather effective if read as a Kafkaesque or absurdist tale.

In the same period, the early 1970s, Will Crowther designed *Colossal Cave Adventure*, 'the first computer-based story that unfolded as you played', and Don Woods, then a graduate student at Stanford, extended it. Of course, this was in the pre-GUI days, when descriptions and actions in computer games took the form of words appearing on or input into a screen rather than of graphic representations but, as Sharples and Pérez y Pérez point out, it is the first link in a lineage that issues in twenty-first-century computer games like *Guild*

Wars 2, *Bioshock* and *Red Dead Redemption* (86). *Colossal Cave Adventure* opened up the possibility of basing a story machine 'not on logic or linguistics but on play in a storyworld'. Sharples himself, for his doctorate in the late 1970s, developed a program to help children expand their writing skills by 'design[ing] their own storytelling games' and creating their own storyworlds, with interesting results, notably the story by 'Sharlene', though similar outcomes might have been achieved by non-digital means. In the 1990s, Scott Turner, also influenced by Propp's *Morphology of the Folk Tale*, produced a story-generating program called 'MINSTREL', which, according to Sharples and Pérez y Pérez 'stands at the pinnacle of AI and story generation' even if, as they acknowledge, its story-range is strongly circumscribed, confined in this case, like a staccato prose version of Tennyson's *Idylls of the King*, to tales about Arthur and his Knights. Sharples and Pérez y Pérez themselves developed what they call an E-R [Engagement-Reflection] model of creative writing as 'an interaction between two mental processes – engagement and reflection – that turn ideas into text and drive composing forward' – and used this model as a basis for their MEXICA 'story-generating system'.

This book suggests many parallels, in the twentieth century, between the concepts and operations of story machines and those that have emerged in twentieth-century literary theory and avant-garde literary practice. As well as Propp's *Morphology of the Folk Tale*, these include Viktor Shklovsky and his Opoyaz group founded during the First World War; Tristan Tzara's 'To Make a Dadaist Poem' (1920); Mikhail Bakhtin's dialogism; William S. Burroughs's cut-ups; and the Oulipo group. These offer, in their respective ways, anticipations of, and overlaps with, attempts to create computer-generated poems and stories. La Salle University, for instance, provides a free online Dada Poem generator, based on Tzara's how-to instructions, where you can paste text into a box, click, and see the result scrambled into a (sort of) poem. Sharples and Pérez y Pérez do not mention some concepts from literary theory that might seem relevant, partly perhaps because they are keen to retain the idea of the (human) creative author as a model for computer creativity. For example, Roland Barthes's definition, in *The Death of the Author* (1967), of a text not as an authorial emanation but as 'un espace à dimensions multiples, où se marient et se contestent des écritures variées, dont aucune n'est originelle' [in Stephen Heath's translation, 'a multi-dimensional space in which a variety of writings, none of them original, blend and clash'], sounds like an anticipatory description of the internet and of the way in which programmes such as GPT-2 and GPT-3 work by collecting a vast repertoire of instances and information from online sources.

It is also striking that, while the authors of *Story Machines* are clearly aware of some key avant-garde literary movements and theories, their narrative aesthetic is largely a conventional one, so that their book shows a not unfamiliar combination of technological innovation and artistic conservatism, although they are familiar with, and show some sympathy for, the Russian Formalist concept of 'defamiliarization'. They tend to be breezily dismissive of the results of avant-garde experiments, for instance in their summation of Oulipo: 'The poets and writers subjected themselves to rigorous constraints to produce mostly impenetrable works of literature'. While their adjectival characterization of Oulipo's products is not wholly unjust, especially to an English empiricist eye, it does rest on the assumption that penetrability is always a virtue, which is not universally the case; indeed, a certain opacity and ambiguity has become part of the commercial as well as aesthetic value of significant strands of contemporary bestselling fiction, big box-office cinema and popular streamed series. As far as fiction is concerned, Sharples and Pérez y Pérez seem to prefer what the post-structuralists called, with their own style of dismissiveness, classic realism. In their accounts of what a story should contain, favourite approbatory adjectives and nouns include 'believable', 'compelling', 'coherence' and, especially towards the end of their book, 'empathy'. This is fine as far as it goes but it does tend to generate the kind of rather debatable assertions we find in this passage:

> To create works of fiction that satisfy human readers requires crafting not only stylish language but also creating engaging settings, memorable characters with believable dialogue, a well-structured plot with mystery and tension, and a great beginning and satisfying ending, all of which encourage the reader to continue reading through empathy or curiosity.

On one level, this is unexceptional advice, of the kind that a middle-of-the-road manual (human or computer-generated), or a course on, say, 'Writing for Pleasure and Profit', might offer students; on the other, it begs a lot of philosophical and aesthetic questions and would exclude quite a lot of the interesting and often important literature of the past and present that aims to resist these easy offerings.

This book's penultimate chapter, 'Build Your Own Story Generator', is enjoyable, particularly as it enables one to play with the 'remarkable paper device to generate new truths through combination and permutation' included in *Ars Brevis*, whose author was the industrious and ingenious thirteenth-century polymath and mystic Ramon Llull; but you might end up thinking that it would be more fruitful and fulfilling to write a story or two yourself. In their last chapter, however, the authors do acknowledge that there is still a long way to go in creating effective story machines, pointing to the irony that John Clark's nineteenth-century Eureka machine could 'generate millions of well-formed Latin verses', but that 'the latest advances in AI still can't compose a coherent story of more than a few paragraphs'. *Story Machines*, however, does sometimes adumbrate an intriguing set of alternative possibilities for computer-generated stories that could avoid the attempt to produce narratives that would be inferior examples, or at best competent pastiches, of classic realist texts and open up new aesthetic and existential possibilities, as it says near the end of Chapter 6: 'What if the computer could write from its own experience of existing and growing within the internet?'. The book returns to this idea in its final sentence: 'If we don't expect computer story generators to perform like human authors and instead design them to generate compelling stories about their own computer-connected universe, then what tales might they tell us?' In this perspective, hearing the voice of the mechanical bard might one day take us into hitherto unexplored zones of innocence and experience.

Communisming
Caroline Clark, *Sovetica* (CB Editions) £10

Reviewed by James Womack

One of the things that distinguishes Caroline Clark's first book, *Saying Yes in Russian* (Agenda Editions, 2012), is her poems' scrupulous and personal physicality. Written largely from the perspective of a foreigner living in Russia (Clark spent the frumious early 2000s in Moscow), several of the poems deal with the minute negotiations between languages, how words feel as much as what they mean. 'Later I mouthed to memory | another [word]: *opúshka*.' The book's title poem records the momentary nasal hum at the beginning of the Russian word *da*, when you could ever-so-easily slide towards *nyet* instead. What this says about the immediate post-Soviet character is hinted at but not belaboured: 'you must surprise [the *da*], yourself and the one who asked'.

The contrast between *Saying Yes in Russian* and *Sovetica* is noticeable. Both are excellent books, but where *Saying Yes* was internalised and exploratory, the result of years of looking, *Sovetica* is more concerned with listening. In his Afterword, David Rose describes the book's technique: 'Caroline started recording Andrei [Clark's husband] reminiscing in Russian about his childhood and teenage years. These stories were then translated into English by Caroline and, with the lightest revision, formatted into prosaic blocks of text.'

The result is a series of almost sixty brief texts, which Rose correctly finds it difficult to assign to a specific genre pigeonhole – 'Poems? Stories?'. More than many other things, they resemble the collections of *anekdoty* that one used to find all over Russia: microstories, occasionally with a punchline, but equally often simple descriptions of events. There, as here, the absurdity of the life described made these *anekdoty* funny, even if the humour occasionally seemed unintentional or oblique to the average Western reader (i.e. me).

The Urtext for such collections is probably the spoof proverbs of Kozma Prutkov, published in the magazine *Sovremennik* (*The Contemporary*) in the 1860s. From Prutkov: 'Throw a little stone into the water, and look at the circles that its fall makes: if you don't do that, then throwing the stone is just an idle pastime.' From Clark:

> In school the idea
> was that when it
> came everything
> would be free.
> Someone would
> offer me a sweet
> and say, You can
> have it for free
> when communism
> comes but for now
> you can buy it.
> When we were
> very small we'd
> steal things and
> say we'd comm-
> unismed them.

There are obvious differences, of course, but the spirit of Russian Zen seems to animate these little koans.

Another possible source that came to mind as I read these was James Joyce's early epiphanies, meticulous recreations of odd passing moments (Oliver St John Gogarty picks up a package from the chemist, &c.) whose value depends on the fact that they are authored and packaged rather than forgotten. There is a very Joycean idea of memory, especially memory-fixed-in-language, as a stay against oblivion that runs through Clark's book:

> There was a point where
> the track forked off in a
> direction I'd never been.
> I wanted to see where it
> went. And whenever I
> passed this place I always
> tried to see further up the
> track. One day I decided
> enough was enough and
> I just got on the elektrichka
> and rode there. I went a
> little way then I walked
> back to my stop.

Of course, there is a world of Soviet suffering and resistance in the story, but the point isn't insisted on: what is important is that Andrei's reminiscences are firmed in place by their transcription and presentation in this form.

A warren of interpretative rabbit-holes one could go down, reading and rereading this excellent book: the tower-block appearance of the columns of text on the page, the decision Clark has made to organise her words spatially; the ways in which that approach mirrors the book's concentration on the physicality of her husband's childhood (there are photos included throughout as well, which also add to the book's insistence on the concrete). But that's for later exegetes. In the meantime, it's enough to simply enjoy *Sovetica's* unrivalled recreation of the thinginess of Soviet life. Give thanks both for and

to Andrei's powers of recall, and Clark's entirely sympathetic transcription of these memories: so specific; so indicative.

Discipline is Stylish

Ange Mlinko, *Venice* (Farrar, Straus and Giroux) $26.00
Reviewed by Maitreyabandhu

Ange Mlinko's poetry extinguishes any lingering claim that rhyme and metre are patriarchal, fuddy-duddy, or incapable of confronting the complexities of modern life. Her formal dexterity combined with humour and tenderness make her the poetic grandchild of James Merrill and Elizabeth Bishop. She has Bishop's reticence and Merrill's Mozartian flare.

Setting up shop in that most demanding terrain, metre and rhyme, it was in her fifth collection, *Distant Mandate* (2017), that Mlinko achieved her mature style. Using received forms to serve diverse ends – war poems, love poems, reimagined Greek Myths – she allowed metre and rhyme to carry her between registers, even between worlds. The fluency of *Distant Mandate*, its wit and pathos, must have been hard won. *Venice*, her new collection (Farrar, Straus and Giroux, 2022) only confirms that achievement.

Mlinko is a comic poet, trying, not wholly successfully, to hide her feelings. Her poems bristle with erudition and wordplay. Her rhymes can be funny – 'A girl puked on the tour bus / on the switchback up Vesuvius' ('Chimera') – or sophisticated: 'primogeniture' rhymed with 'found her', 'parties' with 'nonsignatories'. She can be difficult to the point of obscurity, swooping down on an everyday detail from the heights of gorgeous elaboration. Or she can be painfully terse:

> A ship of cows, en route
> from Uruguay to Syria, sank
> that December near Beirut
> ('Possible Sea Breeze Collision in the Evening
> Hours')

Mlinko combines virtuosity – she is fond of villanelles – with quirky modernity to write about travel, art, roses, pelicans, opera, miniature horses in Florida, impeachment hearings, divorce, and her son's electric guitar. At the heart of her work is a kind of sorrowing cheerfulness. Take 'Piazzetta' (rhymed a b a b c d c d) from her sequence 'Sleepwalking in Venice':

> Canal steps troubled by centuries

and off-the-shoulder things
that scandalize the sanctuaries
lead, among the stony echoings,
to wisdom like *Never send an email*
when you're angry – and never
make a promise when you're happy. (Male
faces grinned.) *We should endeavour...*

'The Gates of Hell', dedicated to Rodin, like the equally impressive 'Bad Form', is a delicate but finally agonised tragicomedy about divorce and child custody. Moving between pentameter and tetrameter (rhyming a b c a b c), it begins:

He didn't mean these kinds of gates.
But here we are. Or I mean I.
On these darkest days of the year,
the sun shows that it accommodates
our needs, and turns itself on high.
Show me, sun, what I am doing here.

Later, the poem links separation (I assume from her sons) with homely comedy:

The sun that cuff-links a hill's white sleeve,
the plane that bootstraps us to the sky,
neither is adequate to the human need
individual to each of us here who leave
someone else behind to cry;
queued, with scarcely a line to read.

Many of the poems are haunted by loss. 'In the Nursery', another sequence, ostensibly about growing roses – 'Don Juan, the rose of love/ (or something like it)' – plays on themes of marital separation and pain, even brutality. The sequence is difficult, gentle and finally very sad. Mlinko is a devotee of Robert Frost's 'ulteriority... saying one thing and meaning another' and Stevens's maxim 'It must give pleasure'. Her poems ask the reader to *work*, as all good poetry should.

If poetry is an event in life translated into an event in language, one without the other will not do. Without an 'event in life', poetry risks obscurity: a conspicuous language-game for the university-educated. Without an 'event in language' poetry lacks energy and intellectual play. Mlinko sometimes slips into obscurity. But her fluency in metre and rhyme helps. If the reader can't always follow her thought (and this reader couldn't), one is always carried along by her ingenuity, enriched and entertained by her vocabulary. Many of the poems in *Venice* are that seemingly impossible thing: an event in language that has become an event in life.

Voyaging Onward

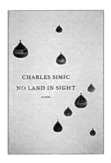

Charles Simic, *No Land in Sight* (Knopf) $28.00
Reviewed by M.C. Caseley

This slim collection is Charles Simic's twenty-third, discounting collected and selected volumes, and we really should know the drill by now: strangely sentient dogs, alarm clocks, a jaunty approach to hell, madness and the afterlife, village idiots, deranged women in cocktail dresses, empty Hopper houses at twilight – a familiar landscape of absurdity in poems becoming ever more minimal. Indeed, the collection opens audaciously with a one-liner, entitled 'Fate'.

The authorial photograph on the back flap of this collection gives further clues, depicting a sweetly twinkling older man with white hair and round glasses, just a little too attentive. Why, he could be the sinister caretaker of the abandoned gothic pile on the edge of town, beside the train lines. In 'My Doubles', he gives a quick self-portrait:

'As for me, the last time someone saw me,
I was reading the Bible on the subway,
Shaking my head and chuckling to myself.'

The valedictory tone of recent volumes such as 2017's *Scribbled in the Dark* continues here, although serious chuckling remains, as does a tone which manages to seem casual, tossed-off, shruggingly demotic – a surface charm strikingly at odds with often apocalyptic asides and insights. This darkness is often dramatised in the disconcerting similes and images: empty clothes hangers click 'like knitting needles / or disapproving tongues' ('Tango'), lovers 'ducking like ducks / in the shooting gallery' ('In the Amusement Park') and all the while, the armless alarm clocks keep ticking. Taken together, there is a sense of foreboding, lit by flames flickering in the distance.

Small single-verse poems do not carry the freight of this imagery often and some here seem very slight: 'A Huge Old Tree' and 'There is Nothing Quieter', for example, both brief pictures of nature, feel a little like flimsy sketches; 'Dark Window' and 'The Young Lady Said' both recognisably inhabit the darkwood of Simic's feverish nights, but both feel a little undercooked. More effective are those leavened with a touch of southern gothic – 'Night Thoughts' and 'Family Graveyard' are examples of this, the former genuinely disturbing, the latter suggesting frenzied unrest continuing beyond this world.
The theological nature of Simic's *via negativa* remains

evident, most obviously in more ambitious pieces. 'Memories of Hell' paints a garish Disneyworld-type experience as surprisingly pleasant, despite incidental fire and brimstone; 'Pyramids and Sphinxes' is almost Borgesian, but with the usual bloody history never far away; 'An Old Woman' is a fine addition to Simic's cartoonish character-sketches. Many of these inhabit, as stated above, the usual surreal cartoon badlands, but two more substantial poems respond to a recognisably contemporary world. 'Celebrity Sightings' depicts 'Tragedy and Comedy / Stepping out of a white limo' into the flashlights and red carpets of Hollywood, archetypes mingling with bouncers in a world of casual dancefloor violence. This is the world of driveby shootings and *National Enquirer* headlines rubbing up against the inevitability of myth. 'In the Lockdown' is even more surprising – the poetic equivalent of Tom Waits singing a straight acoustic ballad after several tracks of lurching, shouted, trombone-led tangoes. In this poem, Simic attests that the enforced withdrawal allowed a reevaluation of internal solitude:

> ...dark nights of the soul
> Thriving in some hole-in-the-wall
>
> Where they found lasting peace
> Obeying a voice in their heads
> Telling them to just sit quietly,
> So that the quiet can teach them
> Everything they ought to know.'

Simic's little boat travels onwards towards the strange lights on the horizon, his idiosyncratic quest still continuing, navigating around the screams and the cartoon violence all around.

Knife in the Ribs

Denise Riley, *Lurex* (Picador) £10.99
Reviewed by Declan Ryan

Denise Riley's new collection *Lurex* is at times abrasive, exposed, off-kilter; it seems often to ask – as 'Air' does explicitly – 'what is the hurt in that light?' There are striking poems which talk about loneliness, but others, too, which use the state of being alone as their setting or their atmosphere; startling, bruising poems, unsentimental but lacerating as we've come to expect from Riley, the great poet of a certain sort of syntactical eye contact. 'One drawback of loneliness: you can notice yourself too much', she writes in 'I get through', but while this sort of close self-scrutiny may well be going on, it's accompanied by a similarly scrupulous noticing of the world, too. 'People

habitually came in twos. Came apart so easily, but harshly'. Life is, in these poems, perilous but ongoing, 'nothing turns 'gratefully' to catch the sun', 'Yet turn it will'. There's a certain Beckettian quality to the poems' focus on the inevitability of the grave ('dear future corpses'), and their insistence on whistling their way there ('The humans sound their billions-fold democracy of distress – a dying spillage. / How clear and plain its songs, how hummable'), their mordant wit black all the way through like seaside rock, the 'two-bit Brit candy' Riley elsewhere co-opts into use in a tribute to the poet Elizabeth Weed.

'1948' is a forceful poem, in fifteen parts, looking at the cruelties and deferred hope of early life for the 'illegitimate sent off to the infertile', the songs made from longing, 'pure wanting, bloodied and radiant' in stark contrast to the 'darling' who 'can turn wolfish', or the harsh treatment and abuse suffered, '*a child has to have its spirit broken, hold your tongue / you disobedient animal*'. All of this takes place in the 'present-past', as the poem's opening section points out, wryly, 'Your past can't tell it is the past. / How to convince it that it's done with now?' Once again, even in the midst of this kind of mining, Riley brings a fastidiousness to bear, not content merely with 'telling... to crack its spell', there's commentary, too, the final stanza a reflection on the nature of this sort of life-writing, the 'apparently personal', as it were, 'a sentence / maybe freeing but only if "done well"?' As the poem's final line has it, 'Judgement runs everywhere in our material'. A hard-wired mistrust of the easy win, or simple gesture, does more than keep her honest, here, it guarantees the second, and third, looks which forbid the pat phrase or unexamined thought.

This is a patchwork book in some ways, there are lots of occasional poems or otherwise somewhat left-handed works collected, some of which don't necessarily rise beyond their commission, or dedication. If it's necessarily less focused than Riley's last collection, the masterwork *Say Something Back*, it feels a little mealy-mouthed to say much about it, and one senses also a deliberate wonkiness to the making of *Lurex*, a letting-off of steam, or at least bleeding of the pipes. As it is, there are still dozens of poems full of surprise, invention, insight. She can still stick the knife in the ribs, as in 'Facts of the 1950s', its sudden lunge into panicked desperation: 'You'd need to occupy yourself throughout this coming sentence, so you invented and rehearsed many silent word games. Though what if you ever ran out of them?' That invention and rehearsal points to something as true now as ever in Riley, of the poem as means of self-salvage, of language as a tool in the hope, however forlorn, of 'a purely secular grace'.

Through a Lens Darkly

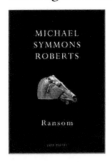

Ransom by Michael Symmons Roberts (Cape) £10
Reviewed by Oliver Dixon

Alongside more common meanings of the word 'ransom' i.e. 'release from captivity in return for a payment, or a sum of money paid for such a release; blackmail', my old OED gives a further definition as '(Theol.) to redeem from sin, to atone for', which links back to the word's etymological roots in the word 'redemption'. One critical angle on Michael Symmons Roberts's most recent collection is to perceive it as caught between these two shades of meaning: between worldly wrongdoing and possible redemption, imprisonment and liberty, the Satan of dishonest money-getting and the Christ who suffered and died to atone for our sins.

In exploring such a rich dialogue, Roberts seems to be continuing the protracted search for possible faith and absolution within a radically corrupted world he has pursued in his previous seven collections. If we accept Geoffrey Hill's parsing of the word 'atonement' as a struggle towards 'at-one-ment' (ie. a unificatory motion), we may also read *Ransom* as a set of attempts at piecing together the debased fragments of 'broken Britain', to navigate a safe path through the scattered debris of our neglected cities and the malevolence and dehumanisation they contain, as well as homing in on fugitive traces of hope in the overlooked and the mundane.

In keeping with this vision, the volume's initial poems transport us into recognisable Roberts territory, with his familiar eye for the defamiliarised *mise-en-scène,* his attraction for unattractive edgelands, 'hypermarket car parks', derelict industrial estates. Through a tense, sinuous build-up of imagery, each poem evokes an air of existential unease and unreality perhaps more akin to European modernist fiction (Kafka, Walser and Bruno Schulz come to mind) than to other poets of his generation. Indeed, some of Roberts's chief strengths are his reluctance to fall back on the default autobiographical setting of so much current verse and in turn his consistent endeavour to elaborate resonant imaginative artefacts which are (in a phrase of Christopher Middleton's) 'shorn of random emotion'.

What's new in *Ransom,* however, is a self-referential quality that plays with a sense of the selfism (or 'selfyism') of our screen-obsessed world, in which the old philosophical idea 'to be is to be perceived' has reached absurd, tragicomic extremes. Roberts, who worked as a documentary filmmaker for the BBC before becoming a full-time writer, employs his keen, ironic instinct for cinematic perspectives and visual effects throughout the collection.

Aside from allusions to classic scenes of kidnap, release and retribution such as the severed horse's head from *The Godfather*, almost every poem contains tropes of representation or the act of seeing reality through a lens or device, from 'the car's reversing camera broadcast(ing) to the dash' and the 'glitch in a game / And I'm just someone's avatar' to the haunting *diminuendo* of 'I Saw Eternity the Other Night', where the narrator looks away both from 'the street outside turned mirror' and 'my TV's illumined bait' towards a dream-world that is itself an infinite recursion of screens:

one vast flawless empty screen
Of screen in screen in screen in screen

Another striking example is 'The Tears of Things', which juxtaposes the supposedly objective viewpoint of security cameras with the 'ultra-foreground' viewed on a phone's camera, a more subjective close-up which seems to make raindrops on the 'wrong side of the lens' resemble 'the tears of things'. Two brilliant, sinister metaphors reinforce this cognitive dissonance of not being able to tell image from reality, or whether internal or external suffering is going on here; firstly an image of unrelenting surveillance:

My neighbour leaves home and walks out of shot,

his progress handed from camera
to camera until the land runs out

Secondly, in a deft semantic twist, 'tears' takes on a different sense, 'not salt but rips', leading to an image of exhausted over-representation, 'the world an old cloth-map of itself, / moth-holed /... blanks showing through all over'. (Perhaps there's a long-distance echo here of a trope from Roberts's 2004 volume *Corpus*: 'the world's pelt / nailed to the picture-rail / of a box-room in a cheap hotel.')

Similarly concerned with multiple viewpoints, the sequence 'Vingt Regards' comprises twenty contemplations or oblique angles on the new-born Christ inspired by a suite of piano-pieces by Olivier Messiaen. The fact that the composer began working on them in Paris under German occupation in 1944 gives Roberts further cinematic settings: some sections feel like excerpts from a *film noir* about wartime Paris, with shady meetings between resistance fighters in smoky bars; others seem to reference *Les Enfants du paradis*, that classic behind-the-scenes drama about Parisian theatre life from the same period. 'By Whom Everything was Made', for example, concerns a set designer's fear that their stage scenery might be seen through as illusion, yet another iteration of the theme of skewed or problematised representation which pulls together this wide-ranging, far-reaching volume.

What would the trees say about us?

Out of Time: Poetry from the Climate Emergency, edited by Kate Simpson (Valley Press) £12.99
Reviewed by Sue Leigh

How might poetry respond to the current climate crisis and the desperate situation in which we now find ourselves? How can it convey a sense of urgency without paralysing us with anxiety? It is a difficult balance. Kate Simpson in her introduction to *Out of Time* describes the book as 'engag[ing] with the power of poetry to ask questions, subvert expectations and raise awareness'. She also reminds us (quoting Roger Robinson) that it is the poet's job 'to translate unspeakable things on the page'. As Mary Jean Chan says of the world of the 'still-too young' in her poem 'One Breath', it is 'too tragic for / silence'.

There have been several anthologies of eco-poetry published this year, including Seren's ambitiously titled *100 Poems to Save the Planet* and *The Ecopoetry Anthology* (of American poems) published by Trinity University Press. The Seren anthology includes work by poets from Britain and elsewhere, *The Ecopoetry Anthology* has a longer historical reach than *Out of Time*, but Simpson's book has a sense of catching the *zeitgeist*.

The fifty poems in this anthology offer a variety of responses, forms and perspectives. Newer voices mingle with more familiar ones. The poems have been grouped under the headings Emergency, Grief, Transformation, Work and Rewilding. (This list might also reflect the journey we have to make in order to deal with the present state of the world.) Their concerns range from overflowing landfill sites, poisoned rivers and frightened children to questions of responsibility, physical work/action and an imagined future in which we might co-exist peaceably with other living things.

We are encouraged to read the anthology as a collection, but it is hard not to single out individual poems. The ones that stand out focus on the particular, enabling us to locate our concern on a scale we can comprehend. These poems use language with precision and freshness. They return us to the world of the senses. One such poem is Sue Riley's 'A Polar Bear in Norilsk' (which won the Gingko Prize for Poetry in 2019). The poem was almost certainly inspired by the image of an emaciated polar bear found wandering the streets of this polluted city in 2019. In the poem we see the world through the eyes of the bear as it asks a series of questions: 'if I could hear the language of sea groaning of ice / if I could turn away from this loud harsh place'. The poem wanders down the page in slow, repetitive phrases – it is haunting in its sadness.

Raymond Antrobus's poem 'Silence / Presence' imagines the sounds of the fossilized forest of Zelandia (a submerged continent beneath the Pacific). The speaker describes how the Tui birds in the Kauri trees 'lioned so loudly / I had to turn off my hearing aids'. This poem also leaves us questioning: 'What would the trees say about us? / What books would they write // if they had to cut us down?' Like Riley's poem, it asks us to see the world from the point of view of another living being.

Other fine poems in this anthology include John Kinsella's 'Eclogue of the Garden 9', in which he fears the abuses of genetics and invasive agriculture – 'I will love the reaching root, leaf / or flower no matter what' – and 'Unripe' by Jemma Borg, which imagines a conversation between parent and questioning child, in which she comforts him, 'What ripens the cone if it is not hope?'

Governmental action is of course the key to systemic change but poems may remind us of what we share, what we put at risk. The plight of polar bear, Kauri tree, garden, frightened child brings the reality of climate change home to us. We must listen. We must act.

Dreaming in 'one discordant voice'

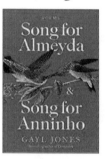

Gayl Jones, *Song for Almeyda & Song for Anninho* (Virago) £12.99
Reviewed by Nell Osborne

Gayl Jones, known predominately as a fiction writer, gained widespread attention in the mid-1970s. She later disappeared from the public eye entirely. In 2021, Virago published Jones's first new novel for over twenty years, *Palmares*, named after the autonomous state in northeastern Brazil formed by fugitive black slaves from 1630–94. The novel is narrated from the perspective of a literate, enslaved black girl, Almeyda, who is later liberated and lives in Palmares as a free woman. Here she meets her husband, Anninho. When Palmares is attacked and destroyed by Portuguese colonisers, the lovers are violently separated. *Song for Almeyda & Song for Anninho* is a poetic companion piece to *Palmares* – or more accurately, both are part of Jones's extensive research on, and imaginative engagement with, African life in seventeenth-century Brazil. The book consists of two distinct sequences. These are narrative poem assemblages; the first features a range of voices in dialogue, whilst the second is a dramatic monologue punctuated with remembered and imagined speech.

Song for Almeyda & Song for Anninho begins with an extract from a historical document, *Petition presented to His Majesty by Domingos Jorge Velho, 'field master' in the campaign against Palmares*, published in 1695: 'It is indeed true that the force and stronghold of the Negroes of Palmares located in the famous Barriga range is conquered... and the survivors scattered... Yet one should not therefore think that this war is ended.' This positions us at a particular historical juncture: Palmares must now be rebuilt from the ground up. Jones's book is divided into 'Song for Almeyda' and 'Song for Anninho' – these missives are dated 1695 and 1697 respectively. In the wake of their traumatic separation, the lovers dream of finding their way back to one another. Despite the implied speaker and addressee of each section, the poem shifts polyphonically. Characters include, for example, King Zumbi (leader and king of the free state of Palmares) and his wives, and an enslaved woman who chose to mutilate her own sexual anatomy (in the place of having no choice, to pre-emptively evade rapacious white slavers). Jones's poems flash with details that are described at length in the novel. For example, the kinds of sexual abuse and mutilation that are meted out to black enslaved women as punishment, misogynistic whim and white jealousy. Almeyda's breasts were cut off after she was caught by the Portuguese. She repeatedly laments: 'Where are my breasts?' Elsewhere, she remembers that her 'breasts were globes floating / in the river'.

One of the driving tensions of the work concerns the place of the love story in a time of violent liberation from colonial rule: '*That was the question, Almeyda, / how could we sustain our love / at a time of cruelty.*' Almeyda's account is, in part, a dramatised dialogue on the virtue of romantic love in a time defined by violent revolution:

What is the right time and place?
Suppose I had said, 'This isn't
the right time, Anninho'? But love
exists in spite of time and place.

In *Song for Anninho,* Almeyda seeks both to record and to recover '[a] legacy of tenderness'. Almeyda travels with Zibatra, a wizard woman, who facilitates 'phantom lovers' visits'. At these moments, the text facilitates sensual conjugal re-enactment as poetic ritual, as if to temporarily suture the divided parts of this history back together.

Throughout, the language is elliptical, taut and prosaic. In *Song for Almeyda*, the short poetic lines are variously indented and capitalised, which lends Anninho's voice a strangely syncopated sensibility:

Wise men seek out wise men as if it
were not wise to
            Congregate
            With fools.

This poem is formatted as a winding channel of text. In the slipstream that is created, certain phrases return with a sense of obstinacy. Overall, the formally innovative elements of this text have an internal logic that can seem rather capricious, even chaotic – Jones utilises italics and citation to build a messily textured story that always remains partial and oblique. Perhaps this miscellaneous approach reflects Almeyda's claim that to write a 'love song':

I would have to make a new voice,
and it would be a difficult voice.
It would not be romantic.

Song for Almeyda & Song for Anninho does indeed present us with a difficult voice. I read the book once before I read *Palmares* and once after and I strongly recommend doing the latter. The novel helps to provide context for the many characters that are only briefly introduced and evoked in the poem. More broadly, however, *Song for Almeyda & Song for Anninho* is crafted from refrains and phrases that reoccur, again and again. Where *Palmares* is a work of extraordinary historical complexity, depth and detail, Jones's experimental engagement with poetics more evocatively articulates the sheers of memory's intensity, recreates its peripatetic drive. Jones is concerned with unlocking something ungraspable through the ritual of orality, the power of spoken language and the heft of its reverberation onwards. Or, as Almeyda's lament reiterates through the words of her grandmother:

I keep repeating myself, Almeyda.
But the repetition is necessary.
What I tell you must stay.

Palmares came out in paperback in August.

Sentiment not Sentimentality

Hannah Hodgson, *Queen of Hearts* (Smith Doorstop) £5
Safia Khan, *Too Much Mirch* (Smith Doorstop) £5
Reviewed by Rory Waterman

I've frequently been impressed by winners of the Smith Doorstop New Poets Prize, as readers of these reviews might have surmised, though much depends on the selector, who changes every year. This year it was Kim Moore, a poet who was 'new' herself not so very long ago, and in this review I'm going to focus on two of this year's winning pamphlets (or, rather, selected ones), both by young women. The cult of newness gripping poetry publishing at present isn't always a good thing: too much comes out too soon, and too many poets are neglected after the first flush of youth, or because they first publish when they're not in it. Hannah Hodgson and Safia Khan, however, feel more than ready. Their particular and individual circumstances might have something to do with why.

Hodgson's primary subject, across two pamphlets and a first full-length collection from Seren, is her life-limiting illness. That simple description doesn't do her justice, though, and the poems in *Queen of Hearts* are usually multifaceted in ways that keep things interesting as well as moving. 'Not All Bombs Get Dramatic Conclusions' is a case in point, witty and horrific at once: 'The foam cubes hiding in the ceiling are liquid-stained', so psychiatrists

> point to the ceiling instead of inkblots. *It's blood* I say,
> *we're below a theatre*. The drains backed up last night,
> and we evacuated the ward. A kid shouted *By smelling*
> > *shit*
> *particles of shit are in your nose*! Until a nurse flushed
> his nasal cavity with saline to shut him up.

Note the subtle shifts in register – 'shit', the prissy but precise 'nasal cavity'. In the poem's last stanza: 'The codeine is fifteen minutes late, and a woman on dialysis / is screaming. *It shouldn't hurt* the nurse says, limping / on her stubbed toe.' 'Still going on, all of it, still going on!', as Philip Larkin said about something else entirely.

Hodgson has an abrupt style, a gift for apposite and unusual images, and an attentive approach to subtexts, which combine to energise some very touching portrayals of love. In one poem, the speaker and her grandmother accept 'the inevitable',

> yet still pretend heirloom cookbooks will fall to me
> > one day –
> that I will birth another beautifully pottered woman
> who'll carry our faces in her backpack, and wear us
> > interchangeably.

In another, and regarding her mother, she writes: 'We operate as a carriage clock, our minds / equal and opposite, unable to touch.' Later in the pamphlet, her parents 'visit, smiling, pain unmedicated, // nor seen or heard. Their lives refashioned, / their souls canvases without painters.' Beautiful, unvarnished honesty. Some poems could be a little tighter: 'What I Wish I Could Say in this Pandemic' is a sprightly list poem, undermined only but crucially by its last line: 'I wish I could say these things, but I can't'. The title had put us there already. But Hodgson is a significant talent, her voice warm yet forthright, her poems emotionally complex yet highly readable, her subject vital.

Safia Khan's delivery is dry – at times extrospective, to use Keith Douglas's term. She is a medical student, and many of the poems in *Too Much Mirch*, her debut pamphlet, show her confronting the new world she has entered – often uneasily, which surely isn't a bad thing for her profession, and which also often serves the poems well. In 'Dissection Room: Reproductive Anatomy',

> The demonstrator is
> using a kebab skewer
> to scrape past strings
> of yellowed muscle,
> tissue-paper intestines
> and shredded labia

For the speaker, a female cadaver is still imagined as the woman that was: 'her haunted eggs / jingle in my brain / like tiny bells'. She is learning how to be coolly practical, unemotional for the greater good, and it's a hard lesson. In some poems, Khan relies on repetition – either to emphasise a point, as in the slightly clumsy villanelle 'Dave', or to hint at routine, obligation, lassitude, as in the intriguing 'On Placement', with its italicised refrain: '*I donned mask, visor, and apron, / washed my hands the right way*'. But in all of these poems about medical practice, the tension is between two mutually exclusive ways in which she should of course respond: empathetically, and with professional detachment.

Other poems concern Islamic faith and childhood ('It was simpler to declare birthdays haram / than explain we cannot afford them'), and the missteps of childhood behaviour. 'Painting Faces' is a longish, perhaps overlong, narrative about partially inadvertent bullying, in which the speaker does not come off well:

> *Your mum is very pretty*, she whispers.
> I barely turn to face her.
> *I've seen her picking you up after school.*
> *She said I can come to yours for dinner.*
> I roll a marble eye in her direction.

The pamphlet then returns to the present. 'Fresh Off the Boat' tells of a man who has suffered almost unimaginably:

> Not enough life jackets,
> he gives the last one to his sister
> who clutches his leg, his body a raft.
> By the time he makes it to shore,
> her lungs are full of salt and ice.
> He holds her limp body all night.

If earlier in the pamphlet we witnessed Khan wrestling humanely with the distinction between the body and the life it once had, here the distinction is fully realised, to the benefit of the poem: note that 'he makes it to shore': she is *not* there, even though her corpse has made it. Now, at night, the man 'stands frying chicken / in the back of a shop for rowdy teens, / who spit out his country on a list of places the UK should invade'. (Surely the comma in the second quoted line would be better placed after 'shop', not 'teens'.) As always, Khan maintains a detached delivery, leaving us to work out what to make of it all.

Contributors' Notes

Jeffrey Meyers, FRSL, has published *Resurrections: Authors, Heroes – and a Spy*.

Peter Sansom's first Carcanet collection was a Poetry Book Society Recommendation in 1990. He won the Cholmondeley Award for *Careful What You Wish For* in 2016, and his new book is called *Lanyard*. With Ann Sansom, Peter is co-director of The Poetry Business in Sheffield, where they edit *The North* magazine and Smith Doorstop Books.

Kudzai Zinyemba is an American poet in her final year of undergraduate studies at Indiana University, Bloomington.

Dan Burt was born in South Philadelphia, read English at St John's College, Cambridge and graduated from Yale Law School. He is a lawyer, businessman, writer and Honorary Fellow of St John's College, Cambridge.

Kyoka Hadano is studying for a Master's in English at the University of Oxford, having recently completed her BA at Cambridge. She is based in London.

Ulrike Almut Sandig, born in former East Germany in 1979, has written five volumes of poetry along with short stories and a novel. She often works with filmmakers, sound artists and musicians. She has won many prizes, including most recently the Erich Loest Prize and the Roswitha prize (both 2021).

Karen Leeder is a writer, academic and translator. Her translation of Sandig's *I Am a Field Full of Rapeseed, Give Cover to Deer and Shine Like Thirteen Oil Paintings Laid One on Top of the Other* (Seagull Books, 2020) was longlisted for the ALTA Translation award and shortlisted for the Schlegel-Tieck Prize 2021.

Eli P. Mandel's first collection of poems, *The Grid*, is forthcoming from Carcanet. He lives in Brooklyn, New York, where he is finishing his PhD at Princeton and training as a psychoanalyst.

Fawzia Muradali Kane is a Trinbagonian architect and poet, now based in London. Current works-in-progress include their collection Guaracara and a long sequence/script provisionally titled 'Songs of Sycorax'.

Miles Burrows is a retired GP, sweeping the garden path. (I keep a corner for endangered weeds, and know the names of all the centipedes).

C.K. Stead's *Collected Poems 1951–2006* was published by Carcanet in 2009. A new collection, *Say I Do This*, will come from Arc next year.

Alex Wylie's second collection, *Krishna's Anarchy*, is published in November; his first collection, *Secular Games*, was published in 2018.

Joseph Minden is a poet and secondary school teacher. His first collection, *Poppy*, is due out with Carcanet in November.

Nicolas Tredell is a writer who has published many books, essays and tales. He formerly taught at Sussex University and now gives lectures, in person and online, across the globe.

Nell Osborne is a poet and researcher, working on women's experimental writing. She co-runs the poetry reading and commission series, *No Matter*, based in Manchester.

Oliver Dixon is the author of *Human Form* and *Who the Hell is Friedrich Nietzsche?* Most recently his work has appeared in *The Interpreter's House* and *World Literature Today*.

Declan Ryan was born in Mayo, Ireland and lives in London. His first collection, *Crisis Actor*, will be published by Faber & Faber in 2023.

Martin Caseley lives in Norfolk and writes essays and book reviews for a number of publications. Recent pieces have discussed Charles Simic, John F. Deane's poetry and Louis MacNeice.

Maitreyabandhu has written three books on Buddhism, two poetry pamphlets, and three full-length collections with Bloodaxe Books. His new collection, *The Commonplace Book*, is forthcoming.

From the Archive

from *PNR* 227, Volume 42 Number 3, 2016

Joy

A dark stage. A woman in a rocking chair. Catherine Blake.
Silence.

They don't want me here... they don't want me...

An old woman, getting in their way,

under their feet.

Look what the cat brought in. An ancient orphan, no future to bless her.

A sparrow, a spider, a nothing.

Good for nothing. And nothing will come of nothing... And nothing will come of me now...
A nothing left in darkness...

This is how it is. This is how it has been always. A parting. [...]

SASHA DUGDALE

more available at www.pnreview.co.uk

Editors
Michael Schmidt
John McAuliffe

Editorial Manager
Andrew Latimer

Contributing Editors
Vahni Capildeo
Sasha Dugdale
Will Harris

Proofreader
Maren Meinhardt

Designer
Andrew Latimer

Editorial address
The Editors at the address on the
right. Manuscripts cannot be
returned unless accompanied by a
stamped addressed envelope or
international reply coupon.

Trade distributors
NBN International

Represented by
Compass IPS Ltd

Subscriptions—6 issues
   INDIVIDUAL–print and digital:
£45; abroad £65
   INSTITUTIONS–print only:
£76; abroad £90
   INSTITUTIONS–digital only:
   from Exact Editions (https://shop.
exacteditions.com/gb/pn-review)
to: PN Review, Alliance House,
30 Cross Street, Manchester,
M2 7AQ, UK.

Supported by